GRUBER'S
ESSENTIAL GUIDE
To TEST TAKING: GRADES 6–9

GRUBER'S
ESSENTIAL GUIDE
TO TEST TAKING: GRADES 6–9

Gary R. Gruber, Ph.D.

SOURCEBOOKS, INC.
NAPERVILLE, ILLINOIS

Published by Sourcebooks, Inc.
P.O. Box 4410, Naperville, Illinois 60567-4410
(630) 961-3900
Fax: (630) 961-2168
www.sourcebooks.com

Originally published in 1986 by William Morrow.

CIP data is on file with the publisher.

Printed and bound in the United States of America.

SB 10 9 8 7 6 5 4 3 2 1

Dedicated to parents and teachers who want to see
their children reach their greatest potential, develop a passion
for learning, and excel in school and in life.

Acknowledgments

I am grateful to the many parents and teachers who kept prodding me to write this book, and to those parents and teachers who reviewed the work.

I would like to thank my own parents, whose inspiration and concern when I was a child stimulated and nurtured my intense interest in helping parents and teachers get their children to reach their highest potential in school and in life.

CONTENTS

MATH STRATEGIES

INTRODUCTION TO PARENTS

As a parent, you are the *only* person who can guide your child through the trauma of the test-taking experience. With the strategies and methods presented in this book, with which you yourself will be fascinated, you can help your child to realize his or her true potential and to score what he or she should be scoring on all standardized tests. The earlier your child learns these methods, the more they will become second nature to him or her and the more your child will be able to use them on upcoming tests and in schoolwork. This book will increase dramatically your child's critical-thinking ability and test-wiseness. *It is probably the most important book you can read and share with your child for your child's future.*

This book has developed out of the thousands of hours I have spent teaching parents to help their children avoid the emotional shocks resulting from low test scores, and from seemingly poor learning potential and low confidence—shocks that can cause substantial and lasting damage to the psychological and educational development of the child. The methods presented in this book are so universal that by the time your child takes a Scholastic Aptitute Test (SAT), he or she probably won't even have to prepare for it!

When I was eleven years old, I scored 90 on my first IQ test, which was far below average. Had it not been for my father, who questioned the low score, and my own eventual development of strategies for thinking and test taking, I would never have become what I am today—"the nation's leading authority on test taking and author of twenty-five books on the subject."

As a parent, you must, likewise, prevent the destructive frustration that your child may experience as a result of not knowing how to reach his or her true potential. Nip that frustation in the bud by showing your child the way to demonstrate his or her true smartness, which every child has.

Here's an example of a question that appears on many intelligence tests and on most other standardized tests. Knowing the correct strategy for answering such questions can make the difference of 30 points in an IQ, determine whether or not your child gets into a private school, and whether or not he or she learns how to think correctly.

Is Column A greater than, less than, or equal to Column B?

Column A	Column B
$7 \times 9 \times 4$	$4 \times 7 \times 8$

If your child multiplies the numbers in Column A and in Column B and then compares them, he or she will take too long and not have time to answer many other questions, or, perhaps, will make a mistake. The thinking strategy is to realize that calculating the products in the columns is *not* the simplest thing to do to solve the problem. And you always want your child to take the simplest approach.

Your child simply has to *cancel common numbers* from both columns, as follows:

Column A	**Column B**
$7\!\!\!/ \times 9 \times 4\!\!\!/$	$4\!\!\!/ \times 7\!\!\!/ \times 8$

And is left with:

Column A	**Column B**
9	8

The obvious answer is that Column A is greater than Column B.

Who knows? If your child masters this and many other such strategies and thinking skills, he or she may become a great mathematician. At least your child will like math and do better on tests. And the same holds true for verbal areas.

A Word About the Psychology of Working with Your Child

Much of the material presented in this book will be as fascinating to you as it will be to your child. However, it is important that your child gradually internalize the methods and techniques and not just memorize them. So you have to work patiently with your child and slowly in some cases.

What you want to do is to gradually build your child's confidence by giving your child the tools and methods presented in this book. But don't rush it—go at the pace of your child. Even if your child grasps only a portion of what's in this book, he or she will be far ahead and make significant progress in school and on tests. This book should get you and your child to truly share an exciting learning experience together. However, it is possible, in some cases, that because of your particular interaction with your child, it may be wiser for you to get someone else (an objective non-family member) to work with your child. You can find the names of such people by contacting your child's school principal or counselor. In any event, I cannot stress how important it is, if you do work with your child, for you to be patient and share your child's excitement at his or her own pace. You will find that you and your child will obtain a truly rewarding, multifaceted experience.

The main purpose of this book is to show you how to help your child to take a test without fear, and how to develop your child's true potential.

This book describes for you, in clear-cut language, the various strategies and critical-thinking skills that your child should know for each of the types of questions found on standardized tests. You will quickly see how effective these strategies are, and you will learn how to answer questions using them. You should demonstrate for your child each strategy presented in this book by working with him or her on the sample questions and explanations given in the Strategy sections. Then, after going over the sample questions, you should have your child work on the additional questions at the end of each Strategy section. You will want to go over these questions carefully with your child to see whether he or she has solved them in the same strategic way that was demonstrated in this book.

In summary: Here's the most effective plan for teaching your child the strategies found in this book.

STEP 1. PARENT: Read and understand the strategies and examples given in each of the Strategy sections in this book.

STEP 2. PARENT: Explain to your child the strategies described in the Strategy section, and then show your child how to solve the various examples presented there by using these strategies.

STEP 3. CHILD: Work on the questions at the end of the Strategy section.

STEP 4. PARENT: Check your child's answers to these questions, and determine whether his or her solutions use the strategies and methods shown in this book. If they don't, explain to your child how to solve the questions using the right strategy.

What Parents Should Know About Standardized Tests

WHAT IS A STANDARDIZED TEST?

By definition, a "standardized test" is a test that is given in the same form to all test takers, and is supposed to measure the same ability for everybody to whom it is given. For example, the test may measure verbal ability or math ability. This means that no matter which child takes the test, that child will obtain a score that measures his or her *verbal* or *math* ability.

The scores in these tests are usually represented in two ways: (1) a scaled score, which is derived from the number of correct answers, and (2) a percentile rank, which lets you know how your child compares with the rest of the test takers. For example, if he or she gets a 60-percentile rank, this means that 39 percent of the test takers scored above your child and 59 percent scored below your child. A 50-percentile rank would mean that your child is right in the middle: that is, just as many scored above your child as scored below.

WHAT IS AN APTITUDE TEST?

Some tests measure *aptitude*, and others measure *achievement*. An *aptitude* test usually has questions that do not require the student to know specific memorizable information such as facts of history, English grammar, science, math, and so on. It usually tests math ability through math skills and logical reasoning, and verbal ability through reading comprehension, analogies, and sentence completions, and vocabulary.

WHAT IS AN ACHIEVEMENT TEST?

An *achievement* test usually has questions that deal with factual information learned in school. However, there is really not a fine line between an achievement and an aptitude test.

HOW ARE APTITUDE TESTS AND ACHIEVEMENT TESTS SIMILAR?

As you will see, one can increase his or her "aptitude" by learning specific critical-thinking skills or strategies, and so do far better on "aptitude" tests. Thus the aptitude test somehow becomes an "achievement" test, since the material tested can be learned. In fact, in recent years some of the test names have actually been changed to reflect this situation. For example, the Aptitude Test of the Graduate Record Examination (a nationwide graduate entrance exam) has recently been changed to Graduate Record Examination, General Test. It is therefore possible that even the Scholastic Aptitude Test (given for the last forty years) may be changed to Scholastic Achievement Test for College Entrance.

In this book we will zero in on the most important and common types of questions on standardized tests. They are:

VERBAL

1. Analogies.

This type of test shows whether your child can reason with words. It tests to see whether your child can make meaningful analogies between sets of words. This is perhaps the best way to test *verbal* aptitude or intelligence. Sometimes the questions also test vocabulary, especially if the words in the analogy or in the choices are difficult.

2. Vocabulary.

This type of test shows whether the student knows the meanings of certain words important to his or her projected level of reading or comprehension. The questions that appear can be in many different forms. *Opposites* of words may be tested; *prefixes, suffixes,* or *roots* of words may be tested. A word might also have to be defined based on the *context* of a sentence.

3. Sentence completion.

This type of test determines whether the child can fill in a missing word based on the context of the rest of the sentence. It actually tests two things: reading comprehension and analytical ability. Vocabulary also is sometimes tested.

4. Reading comprehension.

This type of test reveals to what extent your child can comprehend a reading passage. The question may ask the child to recall specific things in the passage; it may ask the child to infer certain things from reading the passage; or it may ask the child to select the best title for the passage. The reading comprehension question can take on many different forms. Usually a passage from fifty to three hundred words is presented with questions that follow. However, your child may be given only a single sentence and a question about the sentence.

5. Writing ability.

This type of test tells you how well your child can write conforming to standard rules of written English. The questions test whether and to what extent your child knows when and how to *capitalize* and *punctuate,* and how to *express a sentence clearly.* The more your child reads, and the more you talk with your child, the more familiar he or she will be with the rules of English and thus be able to express sentences with good English grammar.

MATH

1. Regular math questions.

This is the most common type of math question asked. It is used to test a variety of things. The question may test how well your child is able to compute or calculate something, or whether your child can manipulate certain math quantities effectively, or how well your child can set up or effectively initiate the solution to a math question. Or it may test how well your child reasons using math rules, and how well your child can translate word problems into math format. These questions can also measure whether your child is able to solve a problem the quickest way.

2. Quantitative-comparison.

In these questions, your child is given two quantities, one in Column A and the other in Column B, and he or she has to make a comparison between the columns. This type of question tests how clever your child is in making the comparison, and whether your child can make a comparison with the least amount of calculation or effort. Logical reasoning is measured, since your child has to determine the most logical way of attacking the problem. In these questions, it is very rare that the child will have to tediously calculate quantities. Usually the child can (or should) manipulate the quantities from one column to another to make a comparison. The child who painstakingly *calculates* everything scores lowest on this type of question.

In all math questions, both regular math and the quantitative-comparison, there are two things that your child must do to markedly increase his or her score, and "aptitude." First, your child must learn the most important math concepts and rules (found in this book); second, learn the critical-thinking skills or strategies that will use these concepts and rules. One cannot be done without the other.

Four General Test-Taking Skills

The following skills will help your child make the most efficient use of his or her time during the actual test situation, when seconds or minutes saved can greatly improve his or her score.

1. CODE THE QUESTIONS

When your child is not sure of an answer to a question, he or she should put a question mark before the question number and not spend much time on the question. Your child can always go back to the question if there is time, and he or she will know which questions to go back to by seeing the coded question marks.

Here's an example: (A check [√] can also be used for questions your child thinks he or she got right.)

EXAMPLE

Choose the word that is closest in meaning to the *capitalized* word:

√ 1. ADMIRE (A) work Ⓑ like (C) set (D) hurt
? 2. VAPOROUS (A) tired (B) simple Ⓒ like a gas Ⓓ hot
√ 3. VAST Ⓐ big (B) simple (C) broken (D) close

You should encourage your child to make as many marks on the question paper as he or she needs to. Many students try to keep their question paper clean. That's a mistake. The question papers aren't graded—only the answer sheets.

2. DON'T GET LURED INTO THE CHOICE A CHOICE!

One of the pitfalls confronting all test takers is the tendency to get lured into wrong but good-looking choices, that is, choices that sound correct. And usually this lure is Choice A, because the test makers realize that that's the first choice your child will see. Here's an example.

EXAMPLE

What is the smallest amount of an American coin that is greater in value than a nickel (5¢)?

(A) 6¢ (B) 7¢ (C) 8¢ (D) 9¢ (E) 10¢

Your child may choose 6¢, since 6¢ is greater than 5¢. That's a lure. If your child reads the question more carefully, he or she will realize that what is being described is a <u>coin</u> greater in value than 5¢. That's a dime (10¢). Your child should be wary and think twice about these seemingly easy Choice A answers.

3. DON'T LEAVE ANSWERS BLANK ON THE ANSWER SHEET

Have your child make sure that he or she never leaves an answer blank on the answer sheet. He or she should solidly mark in the answer to each question:

EXAMPLE

1 (A) (B) (C) (D) (E)
2 (A) (B) (C) (D) (E)
3 (A) (B) (C) (D) (E)

For any answer that your child has guessed at, he or she can always put a question mark beside it, so that later he or she can change this answer. The reason for marking every answer is to avoid the possibility of mismarking the answer sheet, by putting the right answer in the wrong box, because of a skipped answer. Your child should answer every question even if there's a penalty for guessing incorrectly, because the penalty is much offset by the probability of a right answer. Your child should never never leave an answer blank if he or she can eliminate one or more incorrect choices.

4. DEVELOP GOOD TIMING

WHEN CERTAIN ABOUT AN ANSWER

If your child feels immediately that one of the choices is correct, he or she shouldn't spend any time looking at the other choices, but should mark the answer sheet with that choice. However, he or she should be sure that the choice is not merely a lure choice (Choice A). If there is no reason to suspect this, your child need not waste time considering other choices that are necessarily incorrect.

WHEN SKIPPING QUESTIONS

Make sure your child knows that if he or she skips a question, he or she must also skip the number on the answer sheet. Your child should make sure that each answer is marked in the space numbered the same as the question being answered.

TOWARD THE END OF THE TEST

When the exam proctor announces that there are, let's say, ten minutes left, your child should complete all the questions he or she can in that time. If there is some time remaining after all the answer boxes have been filled, your child should recheck the answers about which he or she was not sure. It is permitted to change answers on the answer sheet. However, if your child wants to change an answer, he or she should erase the first answer completely, and then fill in the new choice. Your child should always spot-check to see that all answer boxes have only one answer filled in; otherwise the box will be marked wrong, even if one of the answers was correct. Your child should also spot-check the answers to those questions about which he or she was certain, to be sure that the answer was put in the right answer box. He or she should do this with a few answers; this will ensure against losing a whole string of points because of one mismarked answer.

VERBAL
STRATEGIES

Before beginning to work on the verbal strategies presented in this part of the book, review the four-step learning method described in the "Introduction to Parents," on page 16.

ANALOGIES

Analogies are used on many standardized tests, and many educators feel that analogies are the best indicators of "intelligence" and "aptitude." Analogies require students to think abstractly and analytically as opposed to working out problems in a rote fashion.

Here is a simple example of an analogy:

EXAMPLE 1

CHILD : ADULT ::

    (A) man : boy
    (B) servant : master
    (C) kitten : cat
    (D) actor : director

The question asks the following: CHILD is related to ADULT in which way? The same way that (A) man is related to boy, (B) sertant is related to master, etc.

> ## Analogy Strategy—Always Put Analogies in Sentence Form

It is advisable to show your child the best way of attacking analogy questions *before* he or she learns the wrong method. It is very easy to be lured into a wrong but good-sounding answer to an analogy question. For instance, in the example just given, one might at first glance think that CHILD is comparable to boy, and ADULT to man, and so select Choice A, which is incorrect. Or, one might choose B, because the relation of a CHILD to an ADULT seems like that of a servant to a master. But Choice B is also wrong. And so on.

But there's a fail-safe way to answer analogies without being lured into the wrong choices: *You put the analogy in the form of a sentence and then find the words in the choice that fit the same sentence form.*

In solving Example 1, you would say, A CHILD grows up into an ADULT. Now try each of the choices using the same sentence form:

    (A) A man grows up into a boy. The truth is just the opposite. So go on to B.
    (B) A servant grows up into a master. This isn't true either. Go on to C.

(C) A kitten grows up into a cat. This is true. But go to D to make sure.

(D) An actor grows up into a director. This could be, but is not necessarily true.

So the only answer that fits is Choice C, which is the correct answer.

This sentence method is very powerful, and if your child uses it, he or she will never have trouble with analogies. The method will last him or her an academic lifetime, from grade school through graduate school.

Here's a more difficult example:

EXAMPLE 2

HELMET : HEAD ::

(A) glove : hand
(B) tie : shirt
(C) stocking : shoe
(D) thimble : finger

Note that if you do not use the sentence method just shown, you can easily be lured into any of the choices, since they all sound like they're associated with the analogy HELMET : HEAD. Therefore, the most exact sentence possible must be used, and then all the choices tried with the same sentence.

Here's a good sentence: A HELMET is worn over the HEAD. Now try the choices.

(A) A glove is worn over the hand. This sounds good.
(B) A tie is worn over the shirt. This too sounds good.
(C) A stocking is worn over the shoe. No.
(D) A thimble is worn over the finger. Yes.

So which is the right choice? Since there is more than one choice that sounds good, we must *modify* the sentence to make it *more exact.* What does a HELMET really do? It is not just worn over the head, it is used primarily to *protect* the head from a solid and perhaps sharp object. So we can say, A HELMET is worn over the HEAD to *protect* it from objects. Try the choices now.

(A) A glove is worn on the hand to protect the hand from objects. No.
(B) A tie is worn on the shirt to protect the shirt from objects. No.
(D) A thimble is worn on the finger to protect the finger from objects. Yes!

So Choice D is correct.

If your child understands the above analogy, he or she can understand practically any analogy, whether it's on a sixth grade test or a graduate school test!

Let's look at one more analogy example:

EXAMPLE 3

ROBBERY : THIEF ::

    (A) diamonds : burglar
    (B) hostage : kidnapper
    (C) crime : jail
    (D) forgery : counterfeiter

All of the choices look as if they bear some relation to the capitalized words in the question. For example, you might associate diamonds with ROBBERY and burglar with THIEF (Choice A). Let's get a good sentence: A ROBBERY is committed by a THIEF. Now look at the choices.

    (A) Diamonds are committed by a burglar. Ridiculous.
    (B) Hostage is committed by a kidnapper. This doesn't make sense.
    (C) Crime is committed by a jail. This too is ridiculous.
    (D) Forgery is committed by a counterfeiter. Yes.

Choice D is correct.

There is something very interesting about the sentence method. Even if you didn't know the meaning of counterfeiter or forgery, you could still have got the right answer by eliminating the first three choices.

Most Common Types of Analogies

Here is a list of the most common types of analogies found on standardized tests. It is not important for your child to memorize this list, but it would be a good idea for your child to be aware of these types. Thus when he or she attempts to answer an analogy question, somewhere in your child's mind he or she should realize the type of analogy that will lead to the correct relationship in the analogy.

TYPE OF ANALOGY	TEST EXAMPLE
PART-WHOLE *	LEG : BODY (LEG is *part* of the *whole* BODY.)

COW : ANIMAL
(COW is *part* of the *whole* family of ANIMALS.)

PURPOSE
(what it does)

SCISSORS : CUT
(A SCISSORS is used for the *purpose* of CUTTING.)

COPY MACHINE : DUPLICATE
(The *purpose* of a COPY MACHINE is to DUPLICATE.)

DEGREE
(how much)

GRIN : LAUGH
(The act of GRINNING is not as *intense* [degree] as LAUGHING.)

SHOCKED : SURPRISED
(Being SHOCKED is much more *intense* [degree] than being SURPRISED.)

CAUSE-EFFECT
(what happens)

PRACTICE : IMPROVEMENT
(PRACTICE *causes* the *effect* of IMPROVEMENT.)

SCOLD : HURT
(SCOLDING *causes* the *effect* of HURT in a person.)

OPPOSITE

LIGHT : DARK
(LIGHT is the *opposite* of DARK.)

ADMIRE : DISLIKE
(ADMIRE is the *opposite* of DISLIKE.)

ASSOCIATION
(what you think of when you see this)

COW : MILK
(COWS are *associated* with giving MILK.)

BANK : MONEY
(A BANK is *associated* with MONEY.)

ACTION-OBJECT
(doing something with or to something else)

FLY : AIRPLANE
(You FLY *[action]* an AIRPLANE.)

SHOOT : GUN
(You SHOOT *[action]* a GUN.)

CHARACTERISTIC
(what the thing is like)

SANDPAPER : ROUGH
(A main *characteristic* of SANDPAPER is that it's ROUGH.)

CLOWN : FUNNY
(A main *characteristic* of a CLOWN is that he's FUNNY.)

LOCATION OR HABITAT—OBJECT
(where things are kept or live)

MONKEY : JUNGLE
(A MONKEY *lives* in the JUNGLE.)

CAR : GARAGE
(A CAR is *kept in* a GARAGE.)

USER-TOOL
(what a person uses to create something)

PAINTER : BRUSH
(A PAINTER *uses* a BRUSH.)

PHOTOGRAPHER : CAMERA
(A PHOTOGRAPHER *uses* a CAMERA.)

*All these can work in reverse: That is, you could also have BODY : LEG, ANIMAL : COW, etc., as examples of the type of analogy, WHOLE-PART.

Remember, these examples just given are only for the purpose of making your child familiar with the different and most common types of analogies. Normally when your child attacks an analogy question, he or she will *not verbalize* that the type of analogy is, for example, *purpose.* However, after being exposed to these types, your child will have a better sense of the analogy he or she is dealing with.

Practice Exercises and Explanatory Answers

Have your child try the following analogies (five at a time). Then check his or her answers, which follow the sets of five questions. Go over the answers with your child, making sure that he or she puts the analogy in *sentence form*, as in the examples just shown.

QUESTIONS

1 SCISSORS : CUT ::
   (A) spoon : fork
   (B) hammer : nail
   (C) broom : sweep
   (D) knife : sharpen

2 SAFE : DANGEROUS ::
   (A) wild : frightened
   (B) strong : weak
   (C) long : thin
   (D) angry : sad

3 WATCH : TELEVISION ::
   (A) see : concert
   (B) swim : mile
   (C) hear : head
   (D) listen : radio

4 CAPTURE : LOSE ::
   (A) buy : steal
   (B) push : shove
   (C) develop : destroy
   (D) come : remain

5 BASEBALL : BAT ::
   (A) chess : chessboard
   (B) racetrack : horses
   (C) football : yardline
   (D) tennis : racket

ANSWERS

1   (C) SCISSORS are used to cut as broom is to sweep

2   (B) SAFE is the opposite of DANGEROUS as strong is the opposite of weak.

3   (D) You WATCH TELEVISION as you listen to a radio.
       Note: In Choice A, see : concert, you don't really go to a concert to see it, you go to hear it. Thus Choice D is a better choice.

4   (C) CAPTURE is the opposite of LOSE as develop is the opposite of destroy.

5   (D) BASEBALL is played with a BAT as tennis is played with a racket.
       In Choice A, chess : chessboard, chess is played with chess pieces, not with a chessboard. In Choice B, racetrack : horses, racetrack is not played with horses.

QUESTIONS

6 RAIN : DRIZZLE ::
    (A) weather : forecast
    (B) gale : breeze
    (C) storm : hurricane
    (D) cloud : sky

7 PICTURE : SEE ::
    (A) television : dial
    (B) play : act
    (C) music : hear
    (D) flower : touch

8 SALMON : FISH ::
    (A) cow : meat
    (B) spider : web
    (C) sparrow : bird
    (D) monkey : cage

9 SCALE : WEIGHT ::
    (A) speedometer : car
    (B) clock : time
    (C) oven : temperature
    (D) telephone : distance

10 GIRAFFE : ZOO ::
    (A) buffalo : Indian
    (B) tropical fish : aquarium
    (C) elephant : jungle
    (D) dinosaur : museum

ANSWERS

6 (B) RAIN is much stronger (degree) than a DRIZZLE. Gale (a heavy wind) is much stronger than a breeze.

7 (C) A PICTURE is for SEEING. Music is for hearing.

8 (C) SALMON is a type of FISH (part of the whole class of fish). A sparrow is a type of bird.

9 (B) The purpose of a SCALE is to measure WEIGHT. The purpose of a clock is to measure time.

10 (B) This is a tricky analogy. A GIRAFFE can be found in the ZOO. Tropical fish can be found in an aquarium.

But what about Choice C and Choice D:

An elephant can be found in a jungle and a dinosaur can be found in a museum!

So you have to modify your sentence to eliminate the incorrect choices:

A GIRAFFE (a *live* animal) can be found in the ZOO, which is *not* the giraffe's *natural habitat.*

Now look at Choice B:

A tropical fish (which is *live*) can be found in an aquarium, which is *not* the fish's *natural habitat.*

Look at Choice C:

An <u>elephant</u> (a *live* animal) can be found in the *jungle,* which is not the elephant's natural habitat. That's false—the jungle *is* the elephant's natural habitat. So Choice C is ruled out.

Look at Choice D:

A <u>dinosaur</u> (which is *not live*—the dinosaurs haven't existed for years!) . . . so that's false. Choice D is ruled out! Thus only Choice B remains.

QUESTIONS

11 HAT : HEAD ::
- (A) glove : hand
- (B) tie : shirt
- (C) dress : lady
- (D) cigarette : mouth

12 TENT : CAMPING ::
- (A) house : running
- (B) job : working
- (C) car : picknicking
- (D) rod and reel : fishing

13 ORANGE : FRUIT ::
- (A) puddle : water
- (B) apple : vegetable
- (C) fly : insect
- (D) meat : dinner

14 POOL : SWIMMING ::
- (A) gymnasium : basketball
- (B) lake : flying
- (C) home plate : baseball
- (D) sword : fencing

15 DOCTOR : PATIENT ::
- (A) lawyer : court
- (B) plumber : toilet
- (C) comedian : joke
- (D) veterinarian : animal

ANSWERS

11 (A) A HAT is worn on the HEAD. A <u>glove</u> is worn on the <u>hand.</u>

12 (D) When you see a TENT, you usually think of CAMPING. When you see a <u>rod and reel,</u> you usually think of <u>fishing.</u> This is an analogy of *association.*

13 (C) ORANGE is a type of FRUIT. <u>Fly</u> is a type of <u>insect.</u>

14 (A) A POOL is where you go SWIMMING. A <u>gymnasium</u> is where you play <u>basketball.</u>

15 (D) A DOCTOR treats and tries to cure PATIENTS. A <u>veterinarian</u> treats and tries to cure <u>animals.</u>

You may have thought that B is also a good choice. But in Choice B, plumber : toilet, toilet is not a living thing, while PATIENT and <u>animal</u> are living things. So Choice D is the best choice.

QUESTIONS

16 CARPENTER : WOOD ::
(A) electrician : light
(B) plumber : water
(C) sculptor : clay
(D) artist : picture

17 BOW : VIOLIN ::
(A) compose : piano
(B) sing : guitar
(C) strum : banjo
(D) vibrate : cello

18 LAUGH : SMILE ::
(A) shout : whistle
(B) pull : stretch
(C) hit : tap
(D) touch : snap

19 GENERAL : ARMY ::
(A) pilot : airport
(B) passenger : car
(C) captain : ship
(D) singer : orchestra

20 EAT : RESTAURANT ::
(A) drink : water
(B) walk : road
(C) cook : kitchen
(D) chair : table

ANSWERS

16 (C) A CARPENTER works with WOOD. A sculptor works with clay.

You may have thought Choice D is good, saying that an artist works with a picture. However, an artist paints a *finished* picture; he or she works with *paints, not pictures.*

17 (C) You BOW a VIOLIN as you strum on a banjo.

18 (C) To LAUGH is a much stronger thing to do than to SMILE. To hit is a much stronger thing to do than to tap.

19 (C) A GENERAL is the leader (commander) of an ARMY. A captain is the leader (commander) of a ship.

20 (C) You primarily EAT in a RESTAURANT as you primarily *cook* in a *kitchen.* Suppose you used the sentence, You EAT in a RESTAURANT.

Then you'd see that both Choices B and C work with the sentence. Choice B: You walk on a road. Choice C: You cook in a kitchen. So you would have to modify your sentence to make it more exact so that you can zero in on the one correct choice. You would then use the sentence: You *primarily* EAT in a RESTAURANT. Try Choice B: You primarily walk on a road. No! You primarily drive on a road. Choice C: You primarily cook in a kitchen. Yes.

QUESTIONS

21 BUILDING : CITY ::
(A) office : desk
(B) tree : country
(C) house : lake
(D) restaurant : movie

22 THIEF : STEAL ::
(A) actor : sing
(B) criminal : stop
(C) customer : buy
(D) policeman : watch

23 RECTANGLE : FOUR ::
(A) half : two
(B) cent : hundred
(C) triangle : three
(D) score : twenty

24 MOON : EVENING ::
(A) cloud : sky
(B) butter : toast
(C) earth : planet
(D) sun : morning

25 CAT : MEOW ::
(A) bee : sting
(B) horse : cat
(C) cow : milk
(D) frog : croak

ANSWERS

21 (B) BUILDINGS are usually found in CITIES as trees are usually found in the country.

22 (C) A THIEF STEALS. A customer buys.

23 (C) A RECTANGLE has FOUR sides. A triangle has three sides.

24 (D) The MOON comes up in the EVENING. The sun comes up in the morning.

You may have thought a cloud comes up in the sky (Choice A). But a cloud doesn't come *up* in the sky—it is *in* the sky.

25 (D) This can be a tricky one—you have to find the best sentence, so that you won't have more than one choice that works.
Here's a first attempt:

A CAT MEOWS.
Choice A: A bee stings.
Choice D: A frog croaks.

Now modify your sentence to make it more exact:

A CAT makes a sound of MEOWING.
Choice A: A bee makes a sound of stinging. No!
Choice D: A frog makes a sound of croaking. Yes!

VOCABULARY

VOCABULARY STRATEGY 1:
Learn Prefixes and Roots

Any educator will tell you that the best way to increase vocabulary is to learn the important *prefixes* and *roots* of words. How many words can be learned from prefixes and roots? Well, studies have shown that the following list of 29 prefixes and 25 roots will give the meaning of over 125,000 words. Not bad for learning just 54 items!

This is, of course, just one way to increase vocabulary. The other way is to have your child read as much as he or she can—read anything, from children's books and magazines to newspapers—and *look up words* that are unfamiliar. In the meantime, here are the prefixes and roots:

PREFIXES

PREFIX	MEANING	EXAMPLES
1. ab, a, abs	away from	absent—not to be present, away
		abscond—to run away
2. ad (also ac, af, an, ap, as, at)	to, toward	adapt—to fit into
		adhere—to stick to
		accord—agreement with
		affect—to imitate
		annex—to add or join
		appeal—a request
		assume—to undertake
		attract—to draw near
3. anti	against	antifreeze—a substance used to prevent freezing
		antisocial—refers to somebody who's not social

4. bi	two	bicycle—a two-wheeled cycle
		bimonthly— twice monthly
5. circum, cir	around	circumscribe—to draw around
		circle—a figure that goes all around
6. com, con, co, col	with, together	combine—to bring together
		contact—to touch together
		collect—to bring together
		co-worker—one who works with a worker
7. de	away from, down, the opposite of	depart—to go away from
		decline—to turn down
8. dis	apart, not	dislike— not to like
		dishonest— not honest
		distant— apart
9. epi	upon	epitaph—a writing upon a tombstone
10. equ, equi	equal	equalize—to make equal
		equitable—fair, equal
11. ex, e, ef	out, from	exit—to go out
		eject—to throw out
12. in, il, ig, ir, im	not	inactive— not active
		illegal— not legal
		ignoble— not noble
		improbable— not probable
		irreversible— not reversible
13. in, il, ir, im	into	inject—to put into
		impose—to force into

			illustrate—to put into example
			irritate—to put into discomfort
14.	inter	between, among	international— among nations
			interpose—to put between
15.	mal, male	bad, wrong, ill	malady—illness
			malfunction—to fail to function; bad functioning
			malevolent—bad
16.	mis	wrong, badly	mistreat—to treat badly
			mistake—to get wrong
17.	mono	one, alone	monopoly— one ownership
			monologue—speech by one person
18.	non	not, the reverse of	nonsense—something that does not make sense
			nonprofit— not making profit
19.	ob	against, in front of, in the way of	obstacle—something that stands in the way of
			obvious—right in front, apparent
20.	omni	everywhere, present everywhere	omnipresent— present everywhere
21.	pre	before, earlier than	preview—a viewing that goes before another viewing
			prehistorical— before written history
22.	post	after	postpone—to do after
			postmortem— after death

23. pro	forward, going ahead of, supporting	proceed—to go forward
		prowar— supporting the war
24. re	again, back	retell—to tell again
		recall—to call back
25. sub	under, less than	submarine—boat that goes under water
		subway—an underground train
26. super	over, above, greater	superstar—a star greater than other stars
		superimpose—to put something over something else
27. trans	across	transcontinental— across the continent
		transit—act of going across
28. un	not	unhelpful— not helpful
		uninterested— not interested
29. un, uni	one	unity—oneness
		unidirectional—having one direction
		unanimous—sharing one view

ROOTS

ROOT	MEANING	EXAMPLES
1. act, ag	to do, to act	activity— action
		agent—one who acts as representative
2. cap, capt, cip, cept, ceive	to take, to hold	captive—one who is held
		receive— to take
		capable—to be able to take hold of things

		recipient—one who takes hold
		reception—the process of taking hold
3. cede, ceed, cess	to go, to give in	precede— to go before
		access—a means of going to
		proceed— to go forward
4. cred, credit	to believe	credible— believable
		incredible— not believable
		credit — belief, trust
5. curr, curs, cours	to run	current—now in progress, running
		precursory— running (going) before
		recourse— to run for aid
6. dic, dict	to say	diction—verbal saying (expression)
		indict—to say or make an accusation
		indicate—to point out or say by demonstrating
7. duc, duct	to lead	induce— to lead to action
		aqueduct—a pipe or waterway that leads water somewhere
8. fac, fact, fic, fect, fy	to make, to do	facile—easy to do
		fiction—something that has been made up
		efficient— made effectively
		satisfy—to make fulfilled
		factory—a place that makes things
		affect—to make a change in

9. fer, ferr	to carry, bring	defer— to carry away (put away)
		referral—the bringing of a source for help or information
10. jec, ject	to throw, to put forward	trajectory—the path of an object that has been thrown
		project— to put forward
11. lat	to carry, bring	collate— to bring together
12. mit, mis	to send	admit— to send in
		missile—something that gets sent through the air
13. par	equal	parity— equality
		disparate—not equal, not alike
14. plic	to fold, to bend, to turn	complicate— to fold (mix) together
		implicate— to fold in, to involve
15. pon, pos, posit, pose	to place	component—a part placed together with other parts
		transpose—to place across
		compose—to put into place many parts
		deposit—to place for safekeeping
16. scrib, script	to write	describe— to write or tell about
		transcript—a written copy
17. sequ, secu	to follow	sequence—in following order
		consecutive—one following another
18. spec, spect, spic	to appear, to look	specimen—an example to look at

inspect— to look over

conspicuous—to appear different; standing out

19.	sta, stat, sist, stit	to stand	constant— standing with
			status—social standing
			stable—steady (standing)
			desist— to stand away from
			constituent— standing as part of a whole
20.	tact	to touch	contact— to touch together
			tactile—to be able to be touched
21.	ten, tent, tain	to hold	tenable—able to be held; holding
			retentive— holding
			maintain—to keep or hold up
22.	tend, tens	to stretch	extend— to stretch or draw out
			tension— stretched
23.	tract	to draw	attract— to draw together
			contract—an agreement drawn up
24.	ven, vent	to come	convene— to come together
			advent—a coming
25.	vert, vers	to turn	avert— to turn away
			revert— to turn back
			reverse— to turn around

WORD-DEFINITION EXERCISE— PRACTICE USING PREFIXES AND ROOTS

Now let's see how many words your child can figure out using prefixes and roots. Have your child define the following words by looking back at the list of prefixes and roots. The answers follow the words below.

1 circumvent		**9** sequel	
2 malediction		**10** precursory	
3 process		**11** monotone	
4 stationary		**12** interject	
5 untenable		**13** introduce	
6 convention		**14** recede	
7 revert		**15** concurrence	
8 retract			

ANSWERS

See if your child's answers match these answers.

1 CIRCUMVENT: CIRCUM   VENT
                  ↓   ↓
             around   to come → to come around, to go around
Sentence: The politician cleverly <u>circumvented</u> the real issue.

2 MALEDICTION: MALE   DICT   ION
                ↓   ↓
            bad   to say → to say bad things
Sentence: You are always saying <u>maledictions</u> about him.

3 PROCESS: PRO   CESS
            ↓   ↓
       forward go → go forward
Sentence: How do you want to <u>process</u> this order?

4 STATIONARY: STAT   ION   ARY
                       ↓
                  to stand → standing still
Sentence: The stars look like they are <u>stationary</u>.

5 UNTENABLE: UN   TEN   ABLE
                      ↓   ↓
                    not   holding → not holding, flighty
Sentence: This is an <u>untenable</u> situation.

6 CONVENTION: CON   VENT   ION
                       ↓   ↓
                   together   coming → a coming together, a
                                        meeting of many people
Sentence: Let's go to the computer <u>convention</u>.

7 REVERT: RE   VERT
                   ↓   ↓
                 back   turning → turning back, going back
Sentence: Don't <u>revert</u> to your old ways of doing things.

8 RETRACT: RE   TRACT
                    ↓   ↓
                  back   draw → to draw back (to take back)
Sentence: I'm going to <u>retract</u> what I just said about you.

9 SEQUEL: SEQU   EL
                    ↓
                 to follow → following thing
Sentence: Did you see the <u>sequel</u> to *Rocky III*?

10 PRECURSORY: PRE   CURS   ORY
                        ↓   ↓
                     before   running → running before, going
                                         before
Sentence: These are <u>precursory</u> symptoms of a fever.

11 MONOTONE: MONO   TONE
                       ↓
                     one   → one tone
Sentence: Don't talk in such a <u>monotone</u>.

12 INTERJECT: INTER   JECT
                        ↓   ↓
                     between   to put forward → to put between
Sentence: You always <u>interject</u> your own ideas when I'm talking.

13 INTRODUCE: IN   TRO   DUC   E
                        ↓   ↓
                     into   to lead → to lead to
Sentence: Could you please <u>introduce</u> me to that girl?

14 RECEDE: RE   CEDE
                     ↓   ↓
                   back   to go → to go back
Sentence: The army <u>receded</u> from its front position.

15 CONCURRENCE: CON   CUR   RENCE
                          ↓   ↓
                       with   running → running with, happening
                                         at the same time
Sentence: All these events have a remarkable <u>concurrence</u>.

VOCABULARY STRATEGY 2: Learn Suffixes

Finally, your child should be familiar with the meanings of certain *suffixes.* Here is a list of some of the important ones:

SUFFIX	MEANING	EXAMPLES
1. able, ible, ble	able to	<u>edible</u>—<u>able to</u> be eaten <u>salable</u>—<u>able to</u> be sold
2. acious, cious, al	like, having the quality of	<u>nocturnal</u>—<u>of the night</u> <u>vivacious</u>—<u>having the quality of</u> being lively
3. ance, ancy	the act of, a state of being	<u>performance</u>—<u>the act of</u> performing
4. ant, ent, er, or	one who	<u>occupant</u>—<u>one who</u> occupies <u>respondent</u>—<u>one who</u> responds

		teacher—<u>one who</u> teaches
		creator—<u>one who</u> creates
5. ar, ary	connected with, related to	ocular—<u>related to</u> the eye
		beneficiary—<u>connected with</u> one who receives benefits
6. ence	the quality of, the act of	existence—<u>the act of</u> existing
7. ful	full of	fearful—<u>full of</u> fear
8. ic, ac, il, ile	of, like, pertaining to	cardiac—<u>pertaining to</u> the heart
		civil—<u>pertaining to</u> citizens
		infantile—<u>pertaining to</u> infants
		acidic—<u>like</u> acid
9. ion	the act or condition of	correction—the act of correcting
10. ism	the practice of, support of	patriotism—<u>support of</u> one's country
11. ist	one who does, makes	artist—<u>one who creates</u> art
12. ity, ty, y	the state of, character of	unity—<u>the state of</u> being one
		shifty—state of shifting around
		showy—<u>the state of</u> always showing oneself
13. ive	having the nature of	active—<u>having the nature of</u> acting or moving
14. less	lacking, without	heartless—<u>without</u> a heart
15. logy	the study of	biology—<u>the study of</u> life processes
16. ment	the act of, the state of	retirement—<u>the state of</u> being retired

17. ness	the quality of	eagerness—the quality of being eager
18. ory	having the nature of, a place or thing for	laboratory—a place where work is done
19. ous, ose	full of, having	dangerous—full of danger
		verbose—full of words or wordy
20. ship	the art or skill of, the ability to	leadership—the ability to lead
21. some	full of, like	troublesome—full of trouble
22. tude	the state or quality of, the ability to	aptitude—the ability to do
23. y	full of, somewhat, somewhat like	musty—having a stale odor
		chilly—somewhat cold
		willowy—like a willow

Now that your child has already looked at the section on prefixes and roots, and after you have explained the suffixes with examples, let's see how your child does with these questions. Some involve knowing suffixes only, but others involve knowing a combination of prefixes, roots, and suffixes.

QUESTIONS

1 What is the meaning of tenacious?

2 What is the meaning of irreversible?

3 What is the meaning of precursor?

4 What is the meaning of unidirectional?

5 What is the meaning of parity?

6 What is the meaning of tactile?

7 What is the best meaning of the underlined suffix? director

(A) one who (B) place where (C) quality of (D) full of

8 What is the best meaning of the underlined suffix? anthropology

(A) being (B) the quality of (C) the study of (D) place where

9 Which is the *prefix* of the following word? inject

(A) i (B) in (C) inj (D) inject

10 Which is the *suffix* of the following word? antagonism

(A) nism (B) ism (C) ant (D) onism

ANSWERS

After you have gone over your child's work for the preceding ten questions, describe how to answer the questions using the following explanations.

1 tenacious: ten = to hold   acious = having the quality of
So tenacious = having the quality of holding on to

2 irreversible: ir = not   re = again, back   vers = turning
ible = able to
So irreversible = not being able to turn back

3 precursor: pre = before   curs = to run   or = one who
So precursor = something that runs before or comes before

4 unidirectional: uni = one   ion = the act of   al = having the quality of
So unidirectional = having the quality of acting in one direction

5 parity: par = equal   ity = the character of
So parity = the state or character of being equal

6 tactile: tact = to touch   ile = pertaining to
So tactile = pertaining to something that can be touched

7 The or in director is the suffix that means *one who* (A).
Director means *one who directs.*

8 The logy in anthropology is the suffix that means *the study of* (C).
Anthropology is *the study of man.*

9 The prefix of the word inject is in. Inject means *to put into.*

10 The suffix of the word antagonism is ism. Ism means *the practice of.*
Antagonism means *the practice of antagonizing or hostility.*

Essential Word List for Grades 6 • 7 • 8 • 9

What follows is a list of 268 words. This list was painstakingly derived from the words *most frequently* found on standardized tests, and contains words your child should know. Have your child look up in the dictionary 5 words per day. This list purposely does not contain the meanings of these words, because *your child should get used to using the dictionary,* and discover the meaning of the words himself or herself. Have your child check the words for which he or she has already found the meanings.

abandon
abnormal
abolish
abrupt
absolutely

absorb
abstruse
absurd
abundant
accidentally

acquiescent
adept
adjust
administration
admire

adversary
agility
alertness
allegiance
ambiguous

ambush
ample
amplify
amused
annex

annul
approximately
ardently
assuredly
attain

attire
attitude
audience
authority
aware

baffle
bewildering
bigoted
blend
boast

bountiful
brevity
brilliant

capillary
career
cargo
catastrophe
cautious
cavity
chore

coax
colossal
command
comment
commotion

compactly
complicated
composed
comprise
conflict
constrain

contemplate
contempt
controversy
creep
cunning

curb
cured
curiosity
customary

dally
decent
deface
deficiency
demolish
deposit

designate
desolation
directory
discouraged
disguise

disorder
disposition
disqualify
distress
donate
durable

earnest
eccentric
edible
eliminate
embellish

encourage
endorse
enormous
erroneous
escalate

eternal
evade
evaporate
evidence
exaggerate

excessive
exile
expansion
extensive
fatal

feasible
federation
feign
felonious
ferocity

fertile
festive
filch
flux
forage

fortify
fragrance
frigidity
fulfill
fundamental

global
grandeur
gratify
guarantee

handicap
hesitate
hew
hindrance
humane
husky

identify
ignite
ignore
illiterate
imitate

immaculate
impeccable
impudent
incessantly
inconspicuous

indecision
indicate
inflexible
inquisitive
intention

interfere
intricate
intrude
inundate
invasion

investigate
involved
isolation
keenest
knack
knoll

laudable
legend
leniently
loathe

margin
massive
mature
maximum
meager

melodious
menace
miniature
minimum
moist

monopoly
murmur
negligence
notable
notify

nucleus
obviously
optimistic
orderly
ordinarily
original

parch
particular
patiently
peril

permanent
persist
persuade
petition
petty

placate
placid
pomp
portal
positive

precious
preliminary
premature
prevalent
prior

proclaim
prosperity
protest
provision
query

reiterate
reliability
reluctant
renown
replenish

represent
reticent
revise
rotated

sabotage
sacrifice
salvage
sarcastic
scandalous
seal

sequence
serious
smolder
solemn
solitary

soothe
specific
stationary
strenuous
submit
sullen
swindler

torrid
tortuous
trail

tranquil
travail
treaty
trek
triumph
turbulence

undoubtedly
universally
unravel
urgent

valor
vaporous
vast
venison
venture

verdict
vexation
vigilance
vigorous
violent

vision
visionary
vocation
vocational
volition
volume

wailing
wary
wholesome
withered

withhold
yearn
zeal

SENTENCE COMPLETIONS

Sentence completion questions basically test your child's ability to use words correctly in sentences, that is, to fit the right word to the meaning of a particular sentence (or context). There are essentially two types of sentence completion questions. In the first type, there is a sentence in which a word is underlined and its meaning has to be understood from the context in the sentence. In the second type, there is a sentence with a missing word (indicated by a blank), and the correct word must be supplied.

SENTENCE COMPLETION STRATEGY 1: Try All of the Choices

Here's an example of the first type of sentence completion question:

EXAMPLE

He is not <u>convinced</u> that you can do the job on time. <u>Convinced</u> means

    (A) interested
    (B) daring
    (C) persuaded
    (D) rushed

Here you can try all the choices to see which one fits best in the sentence. That is, of course, if you don't know the meaning of the word <u>convinced.</u>

Try (A): He is not <u>interested</u> that you can do the job on time.
      This is possible but not that good.

Try (B): He is not <u>daring</u> that you can do the job on time.
      This doesn't make sense.

Try (C): He is not <u>persuaded</u> that you can do the job on time.
      This sounds good.

Try (D): He is not <u>rushed</u> that you can do the job on time.
      This doesn't make sense.

So the best fit is Choice C. Note that if you didn't know what the word <u>persuaded</u> meant, you could have eliminated the other choices by this method.

Here's an example of the second type of sentence completion question:

EXAMPLE

He did very well on the exam _____ the fact that he hardly studied.

> (A) despite
> (B) plus
> (C) and
> (D) except

The easiest way to answer this question is to try each of the choices, as you did with the previous example, until you've found the word that seems to fit. For this example, you should know that Choice A (despite) is the right word.

SENTENCE COMPLETION STRATEGY 2: Look for Clues and Key Words

There is, however, a much more accurate method of answering these questions: Look for clues that will suggest the missing word. You can do this by studying the *structure* of the sentence. The sentence in the example above says, "He did well on the exam . . ." and ". . . he hardly studied." You should reason that "hardly studying" somewhat contradicts the fact that "he did well." So the *missing word* is a *link* that describes a *contradiction.* The word/words could be

in spite of
regardless of
despite

You can now see why Choice A fits best.

Here's another example of the second type of sentence completion question:

EXAMPLE

She was really _____ in public, but she was hated at home.

> (A) smart
> (B) silly
> (C) likable
> (D) despised

You can, of course, try each choice in the sentence and probably find that Choice C fits. However, it's a good idea to get used to the more effective method, which uses a critical-thinking approach. The word but gives us a clue that while one thing is happening in one part of the sentence, the *opposite* thing is happening in the other: "She was hated at home"; "she was _____ in public." The missing word must be the opposite of the word hated. Choice C describes a good opposite.

Sentence Completion Exercises and Explanatory Answers

The following are examples of the first type of sentence completion problem. Have your child do these after you have explained to him or her the strategies just described.

QUESTIONS

1 Some items are made to last a lifetime, whereas others are made to be quickly con-sumed.

The word consumed means

(A) to be used up
(B) to be praised
(C) to be eaten
(D) to be sold

2 In order to find out what caused the disease, the doctors had to isolate the disease germs.

Isolate means

(A) intensify
(B) separate
(C) calculate
(D) destroy

3 Because he cheated on the exam, he was penalized by losing 20 points.

Penalized means

(A) gratified
(B) pardoned
(C) supported
(D) punished

4 Everybody understood exactly what he was saying because he gave such a lucid speech.

Lucid means

(A) vibrant
(B) slow
(C) clear
(D) wild

5 John has to travel many hours to his job because he resides far from where he works.

Resides means

(A) travels
(B) lives
(C) plays
(D) comes

ANSWERS

After your child tries the preceding exercises, explain the answers below to him or her, and check to see how your child approached each question.

1 **(A)** "Some items are made to last a lifetime, <u>whereas</u> others . . ." <u>Whereas</u> tells us that others will not last a lifetime. Thus the word <u>consumed</u> must mean <u>to be used up.</u>

2 **(B)** If your child does not know the meaning of the word <u>isolate,</u> it is best to have your child *eliminate* the incorrect choices. Put each of the choices in the sentence:

> **(A)** . . . the doctors had to <u>intensify</u> the disease germs. It is unlikely that the doctors would want to <u>intensify</u> the germs in order to find a cure. Therefore Choice A is wrong.

> **(B)** . . . the doctors had to <u>separate</u> the disease germs. This sounds as if they can then find out about the individual germs—so far a good choice.

> **(C)** . . . the doctors had to <u>calculate</u> the disease germs. You don't calculate disease germs—you calculate the *number* of disease germs. Choice C is incorrect.

> **(D)** . . . the doctors had to <u>destroy</u> the disease germs. You'd want to destroy the germs to make the patient better, but the doctors were trying to find out *what caused the disease.* If they destroyed the germs, they wouldn't be able to figure out what caused them. So Choice D is incorrect.

> Choice B is the only remaining good choice.

3 **(D)** "Because he cheated on the exam," something bad happened to him—he lost 20 points. Thus he must have been <u>punished.</u> He certainly wasn't gratified (Choice A), pardoned (Choice B), or supported (Choice C).

4 **(C)** If everybody knew what the speaker was talking about, the speaker must have given a very clear, understandable speech. <u>Lucid</u> must mean <u>clear.</u>

5 **(B)** If John travels many hours to and from his job, he must <u>live</u> very far from where he works. Choice B is therefore correct.

QUESTIONS

Now have your child try the following exercises, which are examples of the second type of sentence completion problem. (Find the missing word.)

1 Although she is really ____, she does not do well on exams.
   (A) likable
   (B) smart
   (C) rich
   (D) stupid

2 Don't live in a dreamworld— you can't make money without putting in a lot of ____ .
   (A) enjoyment
   (B) happiness
   (C) structure
   (D) effort

3 It's one thing to have ideas, but it's another thing to ____ them into something.
   (A) destroy
   (B) push
   (C) plan
   (D) develop

4 The weather looks slightly gray outside. It might ____ .
   (A) rain
   (B) storm
   (C) pour
   (D) hail

5 That was the best time I've ever had away from home, and to think I didn't even want to ____ .
   (A) stay
   (B) play
   (C) go
   (D) arrive

ANSWERS

After your child tries the preceding exercises, go over his or her work and explain the following answers.

1 **(B)** "Although" is a key word in the sentence. It tells us that something happens even though something else happens. So we are looking for *opposites*. The phrase "she does not do well on exams" makes us believe that she may not be intelligent. But the word "although" in the sentence contradicts that and is saying that she is smart. Choice B is the correct answer.

2 **(D)** If you did live in a dream world, you might think that money grows on trees or that you would have to put very little effort into making money. Choice D is therefore correct.

3 **(D)** The sentence is really saying that it's great to have ideas but you should do something with them. What can you do? You can develop them into something. Choice D is therefore correct.

4 (A) The key word in the sentence is "slightly." If the weather looks only "slightly gray" outside, it then might only rain. It is unlikely that it will storm, pour, or hail. Choice A is the answer.

5 (C) The person is saying that because he or she had a great time—it's a good thing he or she went. So when the person says "and to think I didn't even want to _____," the blank word must be go (Choice C). It couldn't have been stay (Choice A). Play (Choice B) is too specific in the context of the first part of the sentence. Arrive (Choice D) does not make sense.

READING COMPREHENSION (Two Strategies)

Reading Comprehension questions test the general ability to understand what a passage is about. Four specific abilities are also tested:

1. Formulating the main idea:
  To be able to select the main idea in the passage.
  To be able to judge the general gist of the passage.
  To be able to select the best title for the passage.

2. Spotting details:
  To be able to understand specific references or sections in the passage.
  To be able to identify specific things about the passage.

3. Drawing inferences:
  To be able to weave together ideas in the passage to see their relationships.
  To be able to imply things about the passage even though they may not be directly stated in the passage.

4. Identifying tone or mood:
  To be able to figure out the tone or mood in the passage— serious, sad, funny, etc.

Here are some typical questions asked in Reading Comprehension passages:

QUESTION	ABILITY (1–4 ABOVE)
1. According to the passage, the reason why the . . .	2 (or 1)
2. The best title for the passage would be . . .	1
3. Which of the following would the author probably describe next?	3
4. The tone throughout the passage is primarily one of . . .	4
5. The main concern of the writer is . . .	1
6. The word <u>warmonger</u> in line 5 refers to . . .	2
7. The passage implies that John was . . .	3
8. The author's attitude toward Sam is best described as . . .	4 (or 2)

There are two main strategies in Reading Comprehension.

READING STRATEGY 1: Be aware of the four abilities tested above as you read the passage.

READING STRATEGY 2: Using Strategy 1, underline key parts, sentences, or words in the passage so that you'll be able to spot things quickly in the passage when answering the questions.

Here's a reading passage followed by three questions. First, read the passage and answer the questions. Then look at the explanatory answers to the questions. After you have got a feel for how to answer the questions strategically, have your child read the passage and answer the questions. Go over the answers with your child, making sure that he or she answers the questions strategically (as explained in the answers given below).

EXAMPLE PASSAGE

I would give the grizzly bear first place in the animal world for brain power. He is superior in mentality to the horse, the dog and even the gray wolf. Instinct the grizzly has, but he also has the ability to reason. His ever-alert, amazingly developed senses are constantly supplying his brain with information—information which he uses, and uses intelligently. His powers of scent are exquisite. His ears hear faint sounds; they are continually on scout and sentinel duty. Wireless messages from long distances, which his senses pick up, are accurately received and their place of origin correctly determined. It cannot be stated too strongly that the grizzly is not a coward. He has no fear. He is intelligent enough to know that man is a dangerous enemy. He wisely endeavors to avoid man, but if he cannot do so, when the fight comes he exhibits one hundred percent of courage and efficiency.

QUESTIONS

1 The best title for this paragraph is:
- (A) "Characteristics of the Grizzly"
- (B) "The Grizzly in a Fight"
- (C) "Comparison of the Grizzly with Other Animals"
- (C) "How the Grizzly Obtains Information"
- (E) "The Grizzly's Attitude Toward Man"

2 The writer says that the grizzly bear is
- (A) superior to the dog in brain power
- (B) unable to reason
- (C) inferior to the horse in mentality
- (D) lacking in alertness
- (E) unintelligent

3 The grizzly's sense of hearing is
- (A) faint
- (B) fairly good
- (C) acute
- (D) inaccurate
- (E) undeveloped

Before trying to answer these questions, read the underlinings in the passage below and review Reading Strategies 1 and 2, which were discussed above.

UNDERLININGS YOU SHOULD DO

I would give the grizzly bear first place in the animal world <u>for brain power.</u> He is superior in mentality to the <u>horse, the dog</u> and even the <u>gray wolf.</u> Instinct the grizzly has, but he also has the <u>ability to reason.</u> His ever-alert, amazingly developed senses are constantly supplying his brain with information—information which he uses, and uses intelligently. His <u>powers of scent are exquisite.</u> His <u>ears hear faint sounds;</u> they are continually on scout and sentinel duty. Wireless messages from long distances, which his senses pick up, are accurately received and their place of origin correctly determined. It cannot be stated too strongly that the grizzly <u>is not a coward.</u> He has no fear. He is intelligent enough to know that man is a dangerous enemy. He wisely <u>endeavors to avoid man,</u> but if he cannot do so, when the fight comes he exhibits one hundred percent of courage and efficiency.

ANSWERS

1 (A) Throughout the passage, the grizzly is described by means of its characteristics. The best title would be <u>"Characteristics of the Grizzly."</u> Choice A is the correct answer.

2 (A) Here is an example of why it is good to *underline.* Make a note to "see underlined passage above." Your underlinings will indicate that the grizzly is superior in mentality to the horse, dog, and gray wolf. Thus Choice A is correct.

3 (C) This question is more difficult. In the underlinings you can see that the passage says the grizzly <u>hears faint sounds.</u> This doesn't mean that the grizzly's sense of hearing is faint (Choice A). It means that the grizzly's sense of hearing is sharp, or acute (Choice C). Choice B is close, but it is not as good as Choice C.

In summary:

1 Make sure that your child gets the gist of the passage—what is consistently being described. This will give him or her insight into the main idea or title of the passage.

2 Underline those parts of the passage that you feel may be important or required for referral later. The question will not usually repeat or refer to exactly what is in the passage, but it will mention some part of what you read. For example, in question 2 you are asked to compare the brain power of the grizzly with that of the dog. In the passage, however, a comparison was made between the grizzly and three animals (the horse, the dog, and the gray wolf). Also, the word used in the passages was <u>mentality,</u> but in the question the word used was <u>brain power.</u>

3 Often a specific thing will be mentioned, and from this you must *infer* something more general. For example, with reference to question 3, the passage says that the grizzly hears faint sounds. You have to infer that if that is the case, the grizzly must have acute or sharp hearing.

Reading Passages, Questions, and Explanatory Answers

Have your child read the passages below and answer the reading comprehension questions that follow each passage. Then check to see whether his or her answers match those that are given in the book. Also check to see whether your child underlined the passage in the same way as was done in the book. It is not necessary to have the exact same underlinings as long as your child answered the questions accurately. If your child can comprehend the passage *without* underlining and did well with the questions, don't worry about the underlining. You may want to tell your child that it is advisable to underline, in case he or she needs to refer to specific details that he/she normally would not remember.

PASSAGE 1

High in the Swiss Alps long years ago, there lived a lonely shepherd boy who longed for a friend to share his vigils. One night, he beheld three wrinkled old men, each holding a glass. The first said: "Drink this liquid and you shall be victorious in battle."

The second said: "Drink this liquid and you shall have countless riches."

The last man said: "I offer you the happiness of music—the alphorn."

The boy chose the third glass. Next day, he came upon a great horn, ten feet in length. When he put his lips to it, a beautiful melody floated across the valley. He had found a friend. . . .

So goes the legend of the alphorn's origin. Known in the ninth century, the alphorn was used by herdsmen to call cattle, for the deep tones echoed across the mountainsides. And even today, on a quiet summer evening, its music can be heard floating among the peaks.

Now have your child answer the questions, and compare his or her answers with the explanatory answers below.

QUESTIONS

1 The story tells us that of the three old men, the one whose glass the boy chose was the
   (A) smallest in size
   (B) most wrinkled
   (C) first to speak
   (D) oldest
   (E) last to speak

2 One liquid offered to the boy would have brought him
   (A) defeat in battle
   (B) great wealth
   (C) lonely vigils
   (D) another boy to help him
   (E) three wishes

3 To the boy, the alphorn
   (A) seemed too heavy to play
   (B) seemed like a real friend
   (C) brought unhappiness
   (D) sounded unpleasant
   (E) brought great riches

4 The practical use of the alphorn is to
   (A) summon the three old men
   (B) make friends
   (C) call cattle
   (D) give summer concerts
   (E) tell the legends of the Alps

UNDERLININGS

High in the Swiss Alps long years ago, there lived a lonely shepherd boy who longed for a friend to share his vigils. One night, he beheld three wrinkled old men, <u>each holding a glass.</u> The first said: "Drink this liquid and you shall be <u>victorious in battle.</u>"

The second said: "Drink this liquid and you shall have <u>countless riches.</u>"

The last man said: "I offer you the <u>happiness of music</u> — the <u>alphorn.</u>"

The boy chose the third glass. Next day, he came upon a great horn, ten feet in length. When he put his lips to it, a beautiful melody floated across the valley. He had found a friend. . . .

So goes the legend of the alphorn's origin. Known in the ninth century, the alphorn was used by herdsmen to call cattle, for the deep tones echoed across the mountainsides. And even today, on a quiet summer evening, its music can be heard floating among the peaks.

ANSWERS

1 (E) Look at the underlinings. The boy chose the third glass from the last man to speak.

2 (B) Look at the underlinings. The first glass offered (1) victory in battle. The second, (2) countless riches, the third, (3) happiness of music. Countless riches is great wealth, thus Choice B is correct.

3 (B) See the underlinings. When the boy heard the music he knew that he had found a friend, so the alphorn seemed like a real friend to him.

4 (C) See the underlinings. The alphorn was used to call cattle.

PASSAGE

Hatting was one of the first domestic industries to develop in the colonies. As early as 1640, American hats were one of the homemade articles used for barter and exchange. By the beginning of the eighteenth century, hatting had become one of New England's important industries; in the 1730's hats were being exported from the colonies in sufficient numbers to arouse uneasiness among hatters in the mother country and to cause them to exert successful pressure on Parliament for a law prohibiting the export of hats from one colony to another, and from any colony to Great Britain or any other country.

Wool was the principal raw material, but a considerable proportion of the hats were made of fur felt, using beaver fur as the base. The average price of wool hats during the eighteenth century ranged from 40 to 80 cents, and beaver hats ranged from $2.50 to $3.50.

QUESTIONS

1 The title that best expresses the main theme or subject of this selection is:
  (A) "Raw Materials for Hats"
  (B) "Colonial Exports"
  (C) "How Hats were Made"
  (D) "Kinds of Hats in America"
  (E) "An Early American Industry"

2 A law regarding the hat trade was enacted by Parliament in response to a complaint by
  (A) colonists
  (B) Indians
  (C) English noblemen
  (D) citizens of foreign countries
  (E) English hatmakers

3 This law made it illegal for
  (A) Great Britain to export
      hats
  (B) the colonies to import
      hats
  (C) the hatters to use
      beaver fur
  (D) the colonies to export
      hats
  (E) the colonies to change
      the price of hats

4 American hats
  (A) were made principally
      of wool
  (B) did not suit the
      customers in Great
      Britain
  (C) were an unimportant
      part of New England
      industry
  (D) were sent only to Great
      Britain
  (E) were not made until
      1730

5 Beaver hats
  (A) were unpopular
  (B) were much cheaper
      than those made of
      wool
  (C) were made mainly for
      barter with the Indians
  (D) cost more than wool
      hats
  (E) were not exported

UNDERLININGS

Hatting was <u>one of the first</u> domestic industries to develop in the colonies. As early as 1640, American hats were one of the home-made articles <u>used for barter and exchange.</u> By the beginning of the eighteenth century, hatting had become one of New England's important industries; in the 1730's hats were being <u>exported from the colonies</u> in sufficient numbers to arouse uneasiness among hatters in the mother country and to cause them to exert successful pressure on Parliament for a <u>law prohibiting the export of hats</u> from one colony to another, and from any colony to Great Britain or any other country.

<u>Wool was the principal raw material,</u> but a considerable proportion of the hats were made of <u>fur felt,</u> using beaver fur as the base. The average price of <u>wool</u> hats during the eighteenth century ranged from <u>40 to 80</u> cents, and <u>beaver</u> hats ranged from <u>$2.50 to $3.50.</u>

ANSWERS

1 (E) This is not an easy question. Although raw materials (Choice A) was discussed, colonial exports (Choice B) was also discussed. So was how hats were made (Choice C) and kinds of hats (Choice D). Only one of these would not constitute the complete subject. Thus a good title would be (E) "Hatting as an Early American Industry," because the general subject of hatting was discussed as an industry.

2 (E) There was <u>uneasiness among hatters in the mother country.</u> The mother country is England. So Choice E is correct.

3 (D) You have to know what the word <u>export</u> means. Export means to go out from (<u>ex</u> means "out of"). In the passage it says that colonies cannot export from one colony to another, or from one colony to Great Britain or any other country.

4 (A) The passage says that <u>wool was the principal raw material.</u> Thus Choice A is correct.

5 (D) Look at the underlinings of the prices of wool hats and beaver hats. You can see that beaver hats cost more than wool hats.

PASSAGE

The inventor of the atom was a Greek philosopher named Democritus, who lived in about 400 B.C. Even then Greek physicists were wondering about the structure of matter. Democritus suggested that matter is not what it seems—a continuous mass of material. He thought that matter could be broken up into finer and finer parts until finally it could be broken no further. These basic particles he called atoms, something which could not be cut or divided.

We can see for ourselves that Democritus did have a good idea. When a teaspoonful of sugar is put into a cup of coffee, the sugar dissolves and disappears. If coffee—or water—were solid and continuous, there would be no room for the sugar. But since the sugar does disappear, we must conclude that the water and sugar are both made up of tiny particles with spaces between them. The sugar particles slip into the spaces between the water particles.

In one way, however, we have come to disagree with Democritus. Following his lead, for hundreds of years, men thought of atoms as solid little bits of matter. Newton spoke of them as being "so very hard as never to wear or break into pieces." John Dalton, an English chemist, in 1807 called atoms "indivisible, eternal and indestructible."

Today we kknow that atoms are not solid and not indestructible. We now think of an atom as a miniature solar system, with a central nucleus or "sun" around which tiny particles revolve.

QUESTIONS

1 The word *atom* was first used by
  - (A) an English chemist
  - (B) a Greek philosopher
  - (C) an American scientist
  - (D) an advertising writer
  - (E) a Greek physician

2 The author indicates that Democritus' theory of the atom was
  - (A) partly right
  - (B) completely wrong
  - (C) never accepted by others
  - (D) too imaginative
  - (E) contradicted by Dalton's theory

3 Sugar is believed to dissolve in water because

(A) the water is solid and continuous

(B) the sugar is solid and continuous

(C) they are both solid and continuous

(D) only a teaspoonful is used

(E) there is room for sugar particles between the water particles

4 For centuries men believed that atoms

(A) were destructive

(B) had revolving parts

(C) were really unimportant

(D) could not be divided

(E) were like sugar particles

5 An atom can be compared to a solar system because an atom

(A) is round

(B) is unbreakable

(C) has particles revolving around a center

(D) is "indivisible, eternal and indestructible"

(E) is a continuous mass of material

UNDERLININGS

The inventor of the atom was a <u>Greek philosopher</u> named Democritus, who lived about <u>400 B.C.</u> Even then Greek physicists were wondering about the <u>structure of matter</u>. Democritus suggested that matter is not what it seems—a continuous mass of material. He thought that matter could be broken up into finer and finer parts until finally it could be broken no further. These basic particles he called <u>atoms</u>, something which <u>could not be cut or divided</u>.

We can see for ourselves that Democritus did have a good idea. When a teaspoonful of sugar is put into a cup of coffee, the sugar dissolves and disappears. If coffee—or water—were solid and continuous, there would be no room for the sugar. But since the sugar does disappear, we must conclude that the water and sugar are both <u>made up of tiny particles with spaces between them</u>. The <u>sugar particles slip into the spaces between the water particles</u>.

In one way, however, <u>we have come to disagree with Democritus</u>. Following his lead, for hundreds of years, men thought of atoms as solid little bits of matter. Newton spoke of them as being "so very hard as never to wear or break into pieces." <u>John Dalton, an English chemist, in 1807</u> called atoms "<u>indivisible, eternal and indestructible</u>."

Today we know that atoms are not solid and not indestructible. <u>We now think of an atom as a miniature solar system</u>, with a central nucleus or "sun" around which tiny particles revolve.

ANSWERS

1 (B) This is easy. The inventor was <u>a Greek philosopher.</u>

2 (A) Look at the sentence, <u>In one way, however, we have come to disagree with Democritus.</u> This says that he was <u>partly right.</u>

3 (E) Look at the underlining at the end of the second paragraph.

4 (D) Look at the last paragraph, especially the last quote.

5 (C) Look at the last paragraph where it is said that <u>we now think of an atom</u> as <u>a miniature solar system, with a central nucleus or "sun" around which tiny particles revolve.</u>

Writing Ability

There are essentially five ways writing ability can be measured. They are by testing:

1 spelling

2 punctuation and capitalization

3 grammar and usage

4 diction, style, and sentence structure

5 logic and organization

In the exercises below, we will look at the types of questions asked in each of the above categories. However, instead of you or your child having to wade through a set of rules for each category, you are only going to see some sentences that are incorrect, which you will then learn how to correct. You are only going to work with the most important and typical sentences and corrections, so that your child, with the least amount of effort, should be able to answer many questions involving writing rules and techniques.

After you have gone over each of the exercises in this chapter, show the questions to your child and describe to him or her how the correct answers are obtained (as demonstrated in this book).

Spelling

In the following exercise, each question consists of five words. Select the word that is spelled *incorrectly*. If all five words are spelled correctly, mark the answer F.

1 (A) strenuous
  (B) deceive
  (C) salaried
  (D) carreer
  (E) mislaid

6 (A) sophistacated
  (B) predisposed
  (B) taboo
  (D) regimentation
  (E) professor

2 (A) imaginary
  (B) ammount
  (C) homespun
  (D) sluggish
  (E) attic

7 (A) explosive
  (B) galery
  (C) idol
  (D) keynote
  (E) confident

3 (A) tedious
  (B) rellinquish
  (C) peddle
  (D) pasteurize
  (E) dissuade

8 (A) eloquence
  (B) specimen
  (C) beggar
  (D) dazling
  (E) mysterious

4 (A) parashute
  (B) hiccup
  (C) argument
  (D) physics
  (E) opponent

9 (A) plaintiff
  (B) degree
  (C) hostility
  (D) cauterize
  (E) anchered

5 (A) anesthetic
  (B) virtuoso
  (C) consecrate
  (D) afirmation
  (E) alcohol

10 (A) quarantine
   (B) proverbial
   (C) adaptation
   (D) disernment
   (E) stupidity

After you have looked at these questions, have your child try them, and go over the answers with him or her, making the necessary corrections.

ANSWERS

1 (D) career
2 (B) amount
3 (B) relinquish
4 (A) parachute
5 (D) affirmation

6 (A) sophisticated
7 (B) gallery
8 (D) dazzling
9 (E) anchored
10 (D) discernment

Now have your child answer the following questions. Check his or her answers with those given below to see whether he or she has approached them correctly.

Directions: Each question consists of five words. Select the word that is spelled *incorrectly*. If all five words are spelled correctly, mark the answer F.

QUESTIONS

1 (A) renewel
  (B) charitable
  (C) abrupt
  (D) possession
  (E) strengthen

2 (A) khaki
  (B) survival
  (C) laboratory
  (D) intensefied
  (E) stature

3 (A) diesel
  (B) cocoa
  (C) alphabettical
  (D) visible
  (E) overlaid

4 (A) neutral
  (B) ballot
  (C) parallysis
  (D) enterprise
  (E) abnormal

5 (A) ironic
  (B) mountainous
  (C) permissible
  (D) carburetor
  (E) blizard

6 (A) penalty
  (B) affidavit
  (C) document
  (D) notery
  (E) valid

7 (A) provocative
  (B) apparition
  (C) forfiet
  (D) procedure
  (E) requisite

8 (A) terrifying
  (B) museum
  (C) minimum
  (D) competitors
  (E) efficency

9 (A) hangar
  (B) spokesman
  (C) mustache
  (D) cathederal
  (E) pumpkin

10 (A) guidance
   (B) until
   (C) usage
   (D) loyalist
   (E) prarie

11 (A) travel
   (B) conductor
   (C) equiping
   (D) proposal
   (E) twofold

12 (A) philosopher
   (B) minority
   (C) managment
   (D) emergency
   (E) bibliography

13 (A) constructive
   (B) employee
   (C) stalwart
   (D) masterpeice
   (E) theoretical

14 (A) dissappoint
   (B) volcanic
   (C) illiterate
   (D) myth
   (E) superficial

15 (A) totally
   (B) penninsula
   (C) sandwich
   (D) ripening
   (E) salvation

16 (A) pastel
   (B) aisle
   (C) primarly
   (D) journalistic
   (E) diminished

17 (A) warrier
   (B) unification
   (C) enamel
   (D) defendant
   (E) sustained

18 (A) incidental
   (B) lubricent
   (C) conversion
   (D) jurisdiction
   (E) interpretation

19 (A) auxilary
   (B) boundaries
   (C) session (meeting)
   (D) fabric
   (E) ceiling

20 (A) imperious
   (B) depreciate
   (C) rebutal
   (D) wharf
   (E) giddy

ANSWERS

1 (A) renewal
2 (D) intensified
3 (C) alphabetical
4 (C) paralysis
5 (E) blizzard
6 (D) notary
7 (C) forfeit
8 (E) efficiency
9 (D) cathedral
10 (E) prairie

11 (C) equipping
12 (C) management
13 (D) masterpiece
14 (A) disappoint
15 (B) peninsula
16 (C) primarily
17 (A) warrior
18 (B) lubricant
19 (A) auxiliary
20 (C) rebuttal

THE ONE THOUSAND MOST COMMONLY MISSPELLED WORDS

Here's a table of one thousand commonly misspelled words. If your child is weak in spelling, you may want to go over these words (twenty at a time). You may also want to dictate the words (twenty at a time) to see whether he or she knows the correct spelling.

abbreviate	adjectival	anger	asked
absence	admission	angel	assassin
absorption	admittance	angle	assent
absurd	adolescence	annual	association
abundance	adolescent	annually	atheist
academic	advantageous	another	athlete
academically	advertisement	answer	athletic(s)
academy	advertiser	anticipated	attempt(s)
accept	advertising	anxiety	attendance
acceptable	advice	apartment	attended
acceptance	advise	apologetically	attitude
accepting	adviser	apologized	attractive
access	affect	apology	audience
accessible	afraid	apparatus	author
accidental	against	apparent	authoritative
accidentally	aggravate	appearance	authorities
acclaim	aggressive	applies	automobile
accommodate	alleviate	applying	auxiliary
accompanied	alley(s)	appreciation	available
accompaniment	allotment	approaches	awful
accompanying	allotted	appropriate	awkward
accomplish	allowed	approximate	
accumulate	all right	arctic	balance
accuracy	ally(ies)	arguing	balloon
accurately	already	argument	barbarous
accuser	altar	arise	bargain
accusing	alter	arising	baring
accustom	all together	arithmetic	barrel
achievement	altogether	arouse	barring
acknowledge	alumna(ae)	arousing	basically
acquaintance	alumnus(i)	arrangement	battalion
acquire	always	arranging	bearing
acquitted	amateur	arrival	beauteous
across	among	article	beautiful
actuality	amount	artillery	beauty
actually	analysis	ascend	because
address	analyze	ascent	become
adequately	anecdote	ask	becoming

before	challenge	conceive	deceive
began	changeable	concentrate	decent
beggar	changing	concern	decided
beginner	characteristic	condemn	decision
beginning	characterized	confusion	defendant
behavior	chauffeur	connoisseur	deferred
belief	cheese	connotation	deficient
believe	chief	conqueror	define
beneficial	children	conscience	definitely
benefited	chimney	conscientious	definition
besiege	chocolate	conscious	dependent
biscuit	choice	continuously	descendant
borne	choose	control	descent
boundaries	chose	controlled	describe
breath	Christian	controversial	description
breathe	Christianity	controversy	desert
brilliance	cigarette	convenience	desirability
Britain	cite	convenient	desirable
Briton	cliff	coolly	desire
buoyant	clothes	corollary	despair
bureau	coarse	corps	desperate
burial	colloquial	corpse	dessert
buried	colonel	correlate	destruction
bury	column	council	detriment
business	coming	counsel	devastating
busy	commerce	counselor	develop
	commercial	counterfeit	device
calendar	commission	countries	devise
Calvary	committed	course	diary
campaign	committee	courteous	dictionary
candidate	communist	courtesy	difference
can't	companies	crises	difficult
capital	comparatively	criticism	dilemma
capitalism	comparison	criticize	diligence
capitol	compatible	cruelly	dining
captain	compel	cruelty	dinning
career	compelled	curiosity	disappear
careful	competent	curious	disappoint
carried	competition	curriculum	disastrous
carrier	competitive	curvaceous	disciple
carrying	competitor	custom	discipline
catarrh	complement	cylinder	discrimination
catastrophe	completely		discussion
category	compliment	dairy	disease
cavalry	compulsory	dealt	disgusted
cemetery	concede	debater	disillusioned
certainly	conceivable	deceit	dissatisfied

dissipate	*27* erroneous	formerly	hindrance
distribute	escapade	forth	holy
divided	escape	forty	hoping
divine	especially	forward	horde
doctor	etc.	fourth	hospitalization
doesn't	everything	frantically	huge
dominant	evidently	fraternities	humorist
dormitories	exaggerated	freshman	humorous
drier	exceed	friendliness	hundred
dropped	excel	frightened	hungrily
drunkenness	excellence	fulfill	hurries
during	except	fundamentally *27* hygiene	
dyeing	exceptional	furniture	hypocrisy
dying	excitable	further	hypocrite
	exercise		
eager	exhaust	gaiety	ideally
earnest	exhilarate	gauge	ignorance
easily	existence	genealogy	illiterate
economics	expected	generally	illusion
ecstasy	expense	genius	imaginary
effect	experience	government	imagination
efficiency	explanation	governor	imagine
efficient	extensive	grammar	imitative
eighth	extraordinary *27* grammatically		immaculate
eligible	extremely	grandeur	immediately
eliminate	extremity	greasing	immense
embarrass		grievous	importance
eminent	fallacy	guaranteed	impromptu
emperor	familiar	guard	inadvertent
emphasize	families	guest	incidentally
employee	fantasies	guidance	increase
encouraging	fanatic	guttural	incredible
endeavor	fascinate		indefinitely
enemy	fashions	handkerchief *27* independence	
engineer	favorite	handled	indispensable
enterprise	February	happened	individually
entertain	fictitious	happiness	industries
entertainment	fiery	harass	inevitable
enthusiastic	finally	haven't	influence
entirely	financially	having	influential
entrance	financier	hear	ingenious
environment	foreign	height	ingenuous
equally	foremost	here	ingredient
equip	foresee	heroes	inimitable
equipment	forest	heroic	initiative
equipped	forfeit	heroine	innocent
equivalent	formally	hesitancy	instance

intellectual	magazine	Negroes	pageant
intelligence	magnificence	neither	paid
intentionally	maintain	nervous	pamphlets
intercede	maintenance	nevertheless	paraffin
interested	management	nickel	parallel
interfere	maneuver	niece	paralyzed
interference	manual	nineteenth	parenthesis
interpretation	manufacturers	ninetieth	parliament
interrupt	marriage	ninety	participial
involve	material	ninth	participle
irrelevant	mathematics	noble	particularly
irresistible	mattress	noticeable	partner
irritable	meant	noticing	passed
isn't	mechanics	nowadays	past
its	medical	nuisance	pastime
it's	medicine	numerous	peace
	medieval	numskull	peaceable
jealousy	melancholy		peculiar
	methods		perceive
knowledge	militarism	obedience	perform
	millennium	oblige	performance
laboratory	millionaire	obstacle	perhaps
laborer	mineralogy	occasion	permanent
laboriously	miniature	occasionally	permissible
laid	minute	occur	permit
later	miscellaneous	occurred	perseverance
latter	mischief	occurrence	persistent
lavender	mischievous	officer	personal
lead	Mississippi	official	personnel
led	misspelled	omission	perspiration
legitimate	modifier	omit	persuade
leisurely	momentous	omitted	pertain
lengthening	moral	oneself	phase
liable	morale	onion	phenomenon
library	morally	operate	Philippines
license	mosquitoes	opinion	philosophy
lightning	motor	opponent	phrase
likelihood	murmur	opportunity	physical
likely	muscle	oppose	physically
listener	mutilate	opposite	picnic
literary	mysterious	optimism	picnicking
literature		optimistic	picture
liveliest		ordered	piece
livelihood	naive	organization	pigeon
loneliness	narrative	original	planned
loose	naturally	outrageous	plausible
lose	necessary	overrun	playwright
luxury	necessity		

pleasant
plebeian
poison
politician
political
politics
possession
possible
potatoes
practically
practice
prairie
precede
precedence
precedents
precious
predictable
predominant
prefer
preference
preferred
prejudice
preparation
presence
prestige
prevalent
primitive
principal
principle
prisoners
privilege
probably
procedure
proceed
profession
professor
prominent
propaganda
propagate
propeller
prophecy
prophesy
protuberant
psychoanalysis
psychology
psychopathic
psychosomatic

pursue
putting

quantity
quarter
questionnaire
quiet
quite
quizzes

raised
realize
really
rebel
recede
receipt
receive
receiving
recognize
recommend
reconnoiter
refer
reference
referred
referring
regard
reign
relative
relieve
religion
religious
remember
remembrance
reminisce
rendezvous
repetition
replies
represent
representative
resistance
resources
response
restaurant
revealed
rheumatism
rhythm
ridicule

ridiculous
roommate

sacrifice
sacrilege
sacrilegious
safety
sandwich
satire
satisfied
satisfy
sauerkraut
scarcely
scene
scent
schedule
science
scintillate
secede
secretary
seized
sense
sentence
sentinel
separate
separation
sergeant
service
several
severely
shepherd
shining
shipyard
shone
shown
shriek
siege
sieve
significance
similar
simile
simply
simultaneous
since
sincerely
skillful
sleight

slight
slippery
society
sociology
soliloquy
sometimes
sophomore
source
souvenir
speaking
specimen
speech
sponsor
stabilization
statement
stationary
stationery
statistics
statue
stature
statute
stepped
stopping
stops
stories
straight
strategy
strength
strengthen
strenuous
stretch
strict
struggle
stubborn
studying
stupefy
subordinate
substantial
subtle
succeed
successful
succession
sufficient
suffrage
summary
summed
sunrise

superintendent

supersede

✓suppose

✗suppress

sure

surprise

surrounding

susceptible

suspense

suspicious

swimming

syllable

symbol

symmetrical

symmetry

synonym

synonymous

✓tariff

tasting

technique

temperament

temperature

temporary

tenant

tendency

tenet

than

their

themselves

theories

theory

there

thereabouts

therefor

therefore

they're

thorough

those

thought

threshold

threw

through

throughout

tired

to, too, two

together

tomorrow

tournament

toward

track

tract

tragedy

transferred

translate

tremendous

tried

truly

Tuesday

typical

tyrannical

2) tyranny

tyrant

unanimous

unconscious

undoubtedly

unique

unnecessary

until

unusually

useful

using

usually

vacuum

valuable

varies

various

vegetable

vegetation

vengeance

vicious

victorious

view

village

villain

visitor

violoncello

volunteer

warrant

warring

weak

weather

Wednesday

week

weird

welfare

✓wherever

✗whether

which

2 ✗whither

whole

wholly

who's, whose

woman (women)

wonderful

won't

woolly

write

writing

written

yacht

yield

your, you're

Weather

SPELLING RULES

Although the fifteen spelling rules that follow are generalized—and do have exceptions—they will prove very helpful to your child in learning to spell words correctly.

Rule 1

The plural of most nouns is formed by adding *s* to the singular; e.g., *cat, cats.*

Rule 2

When the noun ends in *s, x, sh,* and *ch,* the plural is generally formed by adding *es;* e.g., bu*ses,* fox*es,* bush*es,* bench*es.*

Rule 3

The plural of a noun ending in *y* preceded by a consonant is formed by changing the *y* to *i* and adding *es;* e.g., *body, bodies.* Words ending in *y* following a vowel do not change *y* to *i;* e.g., *boy, boys.*

Rule 4

The plural of a few nouns is made by changing its form; e.g., *woman, women; mouse, mice; scarf, scarves.*

Rule 5

An apostrophe is used to show the omission of a letter or letters in a contraction; e.g., *aren't, we'll.*

Rule 6

An abbreviation is always followed by a period; e.g., *Mon., Feb., St.*

Rule 7

The possessive of a singular noun is formed by adding an apostrophe and *s;* e.g., *father, father's.*

The possessive of a plural noun ending in *s* is formed by adding an apostrophe; e.g., *girls, girls'.*

Rule 8

A word that ends in a silent *e* usually keeps the *e* when a suffix beginning with a consonant is added; e.g., *nine, ninety; care, careful, careless.*

Rule 9

A word that ends in a silent *e* usually drops the *e* when a suffix beginning with a vowel is added; e.g., *breeze, breezes; live, living; move, movable; chose, chosen.*

Rule 10

A one-syllable word that ends in one consonant following a short vowel usually doubles the consonant before a suffix that begins with a vowel; e.g., *fat, fatter, fattest; big, bigger, biggest.*

Rule 11

A word of more than one syllable that ends in one consonant following one short vowel usually doubles the final consonant before a suffix beginning with a vowel provided the accent is on the last syllable; e.g., *commit, committed, committing; forget, forgetting.*

Rule 12

A word ending in *y* and following a consonant usually changes the *y* to *i* before a suffix unless the suffix begins with *i*; e.g., *cry, cries, crying.* A word that ends in a *y* preceded by a vowel usually keeps the *y* when a suffix is added; e.g., *buy, buys, buying.*

Rule 13

The letter *q* in a word is always followed by *u*.

Rule 14

The letter *i* is usually used before *e* except after *c*, or when sounded like *a* as in *neighbor* and *weigh.* Examples of exceptions to this rule are: *neither, either, foreigner, weird, forfeit.*

Rule 15

Proper nouns and adjectives formed from proper nouns should always begin with capital letters; e.g., *America, American.*

Punctuation and Capitalization

Have your child answer the following questions. Go over his or her answers and compare them with the answers given after the questions. Then show your child how to correct his or her mistakes. You may want to explain to your child the directions to the questions.

Directions: In the exercise below, four parts of each sentence are underlined. Choose the letter beneath that underlining where a punctuation or capitalization error occurs. If there are no punctuation or capitalization errors among the underlinings, mark the answer E.

EXAMPLES

1 I want to study law for three reasons, (1) I like the subject; (2) my
                                     A   B

father is a lawyer; and (3) my town needs more lawyers. No error.
C   D   E

Choice A is correct. You use a colon (:) when you are relating something to various items.

2 This is Thomas' recipe for good health: drink milk, eat good sized
             A   **B**   **C**

quantities of fresh vegetables, and exercise every day. No error.
           D   **E**

Choice C is correct. You use a hyphen when two words are linked together: good-sized.

3 George Bernard Shaws play, *Man and Superman,* contains this
              A   **B**

memorable line: "Lack of money is the root of all evil." No error.
         C   **D**   **E**

Choice A is correct. You are really saying the "play of Shaw," so Shaws gets an apostrophe(') after the w: Shaw's.

4 Last year a typical American taxpayer paid the federal government
                 A   **B**

$1,791 in income taxes, $1,103 in Social Security taxes, and
                                     C

$1,920 in indirect taxes such as excise taxes on liquor, gasoline,

tobacco, and air travel. No error.
        D   **E**

Choice E is correct. There is no punctuation or capitalization error.

5 Although Labor day comes in September, my father insists that
              A   **B**   **C**   **D**

every day is labor day for him. No error.
                    E

Choice A is correct. Labor Day is the name of the holiday, so day is also capitalized.

Now have your child answer the questions below. Check your child's answers with those given in the book to see whether he or she has approached them correctly.

Directions: In these questions, four parts of each sentence are underlined. Choose the number of that underlining where a punctuation error or capitalization error occurs. If there are no punctuation or capitalization errors among the underlinings, fill in answer space E.

EXAMPLE

Philip, John, and, Joe went outside to play. No error.
　　　A　　　B　　　C　　　　　　　　　　　　　　　D

Here you would choose C because the underlined part lettered C is incorrect. There is no comma after the word "and."

EXAMPLE

"Don't you understand how to do this?" asked Mr. Martin.
　　A　　　　　　　　　　　　　　　　　　　B　　C

No error.
　　D

Here you would choose D because there is no error.

QUESTIONS

1 We thought he would arrive at Midnight on Tuesday, but he
　　　　　　　　　　　　　　　A

didn't come until Wednesday at about three o'clock. No error.
　　B　　　　　　C　　　　　　　　　　　D　　　　　　E

2 John, come home now, it's time for your dinner. No error.
　　A　　　　　　　　　　B　C　　　　D　　　　　E

3 According to the missing person's report the girl was about five
　　　　　　　　　　　　　　　A

feet tall, of medium build, light complexioned, and wearing a
　B　　　　　　　　　C　　　D

blue and white top with tight blue jeans. No error.
　　　　　　　　　　　　　　　　　E

4 I asked Bill, Jim, and Frank to come with me, but they all said,
　　　　　　　　A　　　　　　　　　B　　　　　　　　C

"no thanks." No error.
　D　　　　　　E

5 Visiting Bear mountain is not too difficult; it's only about a ninety-
　　　　A　　B　　　　　　　　　　C

minute drive from New York City. No error.
　　　　　　　　　　　　D　　　E

6 College Freshmen often work hard studying English, mathemat-
　A　　　B　　　　　　　　　　　　　C　　　　D

ics, science, history, and foreign languages. No error.
　　　　　　　　　　　　　　　　　　E

7 "Didnt I tell you I'd wait for you on the east side of Broadway?"
　　A　　　　　　B　　　　　　　　　　　　C　　　D

she yelled angrily. No error.
　　　　　　　　E

8 The tall, handsome actor on the stage is my brother; He's the star
     A   B   C
of the show and its most popular performer. No error.
                    D   E

9 If I'm not there on time Tuesday, it'll be because I'll have
                           A   B C   D
changed my mind about going to the Caribbean. No error.
                                              E

10 "Bang on the door," advised the policeman, "and he will wake up
                 A   B   C
(I hope)". No error.
    D   E

ANSWERS

1 (A) midnight
2 (B) now; *or* now. It's
3 (A) report, the
4 (D) "No
5 (B) Mountain

6 (B) freshmen
7 (A) Didn't
8 (C) he's
9 (E) No error
10 (D) (I hope)."

Grammar and Correct Usage

Have your child answer the following questions. Go over his or her answers and compare them with the answers given after the questions. Then show your child how to correct his or her mistakes. You may want to explain to your child the directions to the questions.

Directions: In each of the questions below, you will find a sentence with four words (or phrases) underlined. In some sentences one of the underlined words (or phrases) is incorrect according to the rules of standard written English for grammar and correct usage. No sentence has more than one error. You are to assume that the rest of the sentence (whatever is not underlined) is correct. If you find an error, choose the letter of the underlined word (or phrase) that is incorrect. If you find no error, mark the answer E.

EXAMPLE

1 Since oxygen is necessary for human life, scientists are exploring
                   A   B
the possibility of providing oxygen for future inhabitants of space
                   C   D
stations. No error.
          E

Choice E is correct. There is no grammar or usage error.

2 Its my opinion that learning the correct pronunciation of a word
   A   B

should precede any attempt to learn the correct spelling. No error.
      C   D   E

Choice A is correct. This should read, "It's my opinion . . ."

A contraction is needed here. (*It's* means *It is*.)

3 If I would have known more about the person whom I was writing
       A   B   C

to, I would have written a better answer. No error.
                    D   E

Choice A is correct. This should read, "If I had known . . ."

The "if clause" of the past contrary-to-fact conditional statement
requires the *had known* form—not the *would have known* form.

4 If you compare Bill and Joe as far as scholarship goes, you will
        A   B

have to conclude that Bill is, without any question, the brightest.
                        C   D

No error.
  E

Choice D is correct. This should read, ". . . Bill is, without any
question, the brighter."
When comparing two individuals, we use the comparative form
(*brighter*)—not the superlative form (*brightest*).

5 In spite of how very poor Ellen had done in the art competition,
      A   B   C

she was far from discouraged. No error.
       D   E

Choice B is correct. This should read, "In spite of how poorly . . ."
The adverb (*poorly*)—not the adjective (*poor*)—must be used to
modify the verb (*had done*).

Now have your child answer the questions below. Check your
child's answers with those given in the book to see whether he or
she has approached them correctly.

Directions: In each of the following questions, you will find a sentence with four words (or phrases) underlined. In some sentences
one of the underlined words (or phrases) is incorrect according to
the rules of standard written English for grammar and correct usage.

No sentence has more than one error. You are to assume that the rest of the sentence (whatever is not underlined) is correct. If you find an error, choose the letter of the underlined word (or phrase) that is incorrect. If you find no error, mark the answer E.

EXAMPLE

They is coming to the party tomorrow night. No error.
A B   C   D   E

Here you would choose A, because the underlined part lettered A is incorrect.

EXAMPLE

John and I were very happy when we found out our scores on the
A   B   C   D

test. No error.
E

Here you would choose E, because there is no error.

QUESTIONS

1 The man who's temper is under control at all times is more likely
A   B   C   D

to think clearly and to achieve success in his business and social

relations. No error.
E

2 Whether nineteenth-century classics should be taught in school
A

today has become a matter of controversy for students and teach-
B   C

ers alike. No error.
D   E

3 Neither George Foreman or millions of others believed that
A   B

Muhammad Ali would win the heavyweight title by an
C

eighth-round knockout. No error.
D   E

4 Bob wanted to finish his homework completely before his
A   B

mother had come home from her sister's house. No error.
C   D   E

5 Inflation together with the high interest rates and soaring prices
A

are hurting some nations' economy very seriously. No error.
B   C   D   E

6 The Pirates <u>lost</u> the game against the Dodgers because Smith <u>hit</u> a
            A   B

home run with the bases <u>full</u> and played <u>beautiful</u> in the outfield.
                         C   D

<u>No error.</u>
     E

7 The Watergate scandal <u>may be</u> a thing <u>of the past</u> but the Repub-
                            A   B

licans will feel <u>it's</u> <u>effects</u> for a long time to come. <u>No error.</u>
                 C   D   E

8 If we <u>had began</u> our vacation a day <u>earlier,</u> we <u>wouldn't have had</u>
            A   B   C

so much trouble <u>getting</u> a plane reservation. <u>No error.</u>
                D   E

9 We're <u>sure</u> that Chris Evert Lloyd and Tracy Austin are <u>both</u> great
            A   B

tennis players, but <u>who's</u> to judge which one is the <u>best</u> of the
                    C   D

two? <u>No error.</u>
         E

10 All of the class <u>presidents</u> but Jerry, Alice, and <u>I</u> were <u>at the meet</u>
                        A   B   C

ing to select the delegates for next <u>month's</u> convention. <u>No error.</u>
                                     D   E

ANSWERS

1 (A) "The man <u>whose</u> temper is under control . . ."
       The contraction *(who's* meaning *who is)* is obviously in-
       correct here. We need the possessive pronoun-adjective
       whose to modify the noun *(temper).*

2 (E) All underlined parts are correct.

3 (A) "Neither George Foreman <u>nor</u> millions of others . . ."
       Neither must be paired with *nor* (not with *or).*

4 (C) ". . . before his mother <u>came</u> home . . ."
       The past perfect tense *(had come)* is used for a past action
       that occurs before another past action. The mother's coming
       home did not occur before Bob wanted to finish his home-
       work. Therefore, the past tense *(came)* should be used—not
       the past perfect tense *(had come).*

5 (B) "Inflation together with the high interest rates and soaring prices is hurting . . ."

The subject of the sentence is *inflation*. This is a singular subject, so the verb must be singular—*is hurting* (not *are hurting*). The words *rates* and *prices* are not parts of the subject.

6 (D) ". . . played beautifully in the outfield."

The adverb *(beautifully)*—not the adjective *(beautiful)*—must be used to modify the verb *(played)*.

7 (C) ". . . the Republicans will feel its effects . . ."

The possessive pronoun-adjective *its* does not have an apostrophe. There is another word *it's,* which means *it is.*

8 (A) "If we had begun our vacation . . ."

The past perfect tense of *to begin* is *had begun*—not *had began.*

9 (D) ". . . which one is the better of the two?"

In comparing two persons or things, we use the comparative degree *(better)*—not the superlative degree *(best).*

10 (B) "All of the class presidents but Jerry, Alice, and me . . ."

The preposition *(but)* must take an object form *(me)*—not a subject form *(I).*

Choosing the Right Word

The difference between the right word and the almost-right word is the difference between lightning and the lightning bug (firefly).

—Mark Twain

Here is a list of words that are commonly misused. You may want to look through the list yourself and then explain some of the misuses to your child. It should be kept as a reference so that you can check from time to time to see whether your child is misusing a word.

A, AN. The indefinite article *a* is used before a consonant sound; the indefinite article *an* is used before a vowel sound. Say *a plan, an idea.*

ACCEPT, EXCEPT. *Accept* means *to receive; except* when used as a verb means *to leave out.* (We *accepted* the gift. Pedro's name was *excepted* from the honor roll.) The word *except* is used most often as a preposition. *Everyone went except me.*

AFFECT, EFFECT. *Affect* is a verb that means to *influence.* (Winning the sweepstakes will *affect* his attitude.) *Effect,* as a noun, means *an influence.* (Smoking has an *effect* on one's health.) *Effect,* as a verb, means to *bring about.* (The teacher's praise *effected* a change in the student.)

Affected, as an adjective, has the meaning of *false.* (She had an *affected* way of speaking.)

AGGRAVATE, IRRITATE. *Aggravate* means to make worse. (Drinking ice water will *aggravate* your cold.) *Irritate* means to *annoy* or *exasperate.* (Mary's continuous chattering *irritated* me.)

AIN'T. Do not use this expression.

ALREADY, ALL READY. *Already* means *before* or *by a certain time.* (Mike said that he had *already* done the job.) *All ready* means *completely ready.* (When the buzzer sounded, the horses were *all ready* to start running.)

ALL RIGHT, ALRIGHT. The only correct spelling is *all right.*

ALTOGETHER, ALL TOGETHER. *Altogether* means *entirely, wholly.* (Jane is *altogether* too conceited to get along with people.) *All together* means *as a group.* (After the explosion, the boss was relieved to find his workers *all together* in front of the building.)

AMONG, BETWEEN. *Among* is used with more than two persons or things. (The manager distributed the gifts *among* all of the employees.) *Between* is used only with two persons or things. (The steak was divided *between the two children.*)

AMOUNT, NUMBER. *Amount* is used to refer to things in bulk. (The war costs a great *amount* of money.) *Number* is used to refer to things that can be counted. (A large *number* of pupils attend this school.)

AND ETC. This is incorrect. The abbreviation *etc.* stands for the Latin *et cetera.* The *et* means *and;* the *cetera* means *other things.* It is wrong to say *and etc.* because the idea of *and* is already included in the *etc.*

ANYWAYS, ANYWHERES, EVERYWHERES, SOMEWHERES. These expressions are not correct. Omit the final *s* after each.

AS, LIKE. *As,* used as a conjunction, is followed by a verb. (Please do it *as* I told you to.) *Like* may not be used as a conjunction. If it is used as a preposition, it is not followed by a verb. (This ice cream looks *like* custard.)

AWFUL. See **TERRIFIC, TERRIBLE.**

BEING THAT. *Being that* is incorrect when used to mean *since* or *because.* (*Since* you are tired, you ought to rest.)

BESIDE, BESIDES. *Beside* means *alongside of; besides* means *in addition to.* (Nixon sat *beside* Autry at the baseball game.) There is nobody *besides* her husband who understands Ann.)

BETWEEN. See **AMONG.**

BRING, TAKE. Consider the speaker as a starting point. *Bring* is used for something carried in the direction of the speaker. (When you return from lunch, please *bring* me a ham sandwich.) *Take* is used for something carried away from the speaker. (If you are going downtown, please *take* this letter to the post office.)

BUNCH. *Bunch* means cluster. Do no use *bunch* for group or crowd. (This is a large *bunch* of grapes.) (A *crowd* of people were at the scene of the accident.)

BUT THAT, BUT WHAT. Do not use these expressions in place of *that* in structures like the following: I do not question *that* (not *but that)* you are richer than I am.

CAN'T HARDLY. Don't use this double negative. Say *can hardly.*

CONTINUAL, CONTINUOUS. *Continual* means happening at intervals. (Salesmen are *continually* walking into this office.) *Continuous* means going on without interruption. (Without a moment of dry weather, it rained *continuously* for forty days and forty nights.)

COULD OF. Do not use for *could have.*

DATA. Although *data* is the plural of *datum,* idiom permits the use of this word as a singular. Some authorities still insist on *Data are gathered* rather than *Data is gathered* or *these data* rather than *this data.* Most persons in computer programming now say *Data is gathered* or *this data.*

DEAL. Do not use this term for *arrangement* or *transaction.* (He has an *excellent arrangement* (not *deal*) with the manager.)

DIFFERENT FROM, DIFFERENT THAN. *Different from* is correct. *Different than* is incorrect. (His method of doing this is *different from* mine.)

DISCOVER, INVENT. *Discover* means to see or learn something that has not been previously known. (They say the Vikings, not Columbus, *discovered* America.) *Invent* means to create for the first time. (William S. Burroughs *invented* the adding machine.)

DISINTERESTED, UNINTERESTED. *Disinterested* means without bias. (An umpire must be *disinterested* to judge fairly in a baseball game.) *Uninterested* means not caring about a situation. (I am totally *uninterested* in your plan.)

DOESN'T, DON'T. *Doesn't* means *does not; don't* means *do not.* Do not say *He don't (do not)* when you mean *He doesn't (does not).*

DUE TO. At the beginning of a sentence, *due to* is always incorrect. Use, instead, *on account of, because of,* or a similar expression. (*On account of* bad weather, the contest was postponed.) As a predicate adjective construction, *due to* is correct. His weakness was *due* to his hunger.

EACH OTHER, ONE ANOTHER. *Each other* is used for two persons. (The executive and his secretary antagonize *each other.*) *One another* is used for more than two persons. The members of the large family love *one another.)*

EFFECT. See **AFFECT.**

ENTHUSE. Do not use this word. Say *enthusiastic.* (The art critic was *enthusiastic* about the painting.)

EQUALLY AS GOOD. This expression is incorrect. Say, instead, *just as good.* (This car is *just as good* as that.)

FARTHER, FURTHER. *Farther* is used for a distance that is measurable. (The farmer's house is about 100 yards *farther* down the road.) *Further* is used to express the extension of an idea. (A *further* explanation may be necessary.)

FEWER, LESS. *Fewer* applies to what may be counted. (Greenwich Village has *fewer* conservatives than liberals.) *Less* refers to degree or amount. *(Less* rain fell this month than the month before.)

FLOUT, FLAUNT. *Flout* means to mock or insult. (The king *flouted* the wise man when the latter offered advice.) *Flaunt* means to make a pretentious display of. (The upstart *flaunted* his diamond ring.)

FURTHER. See **FARTHER.**

GET. *Get* means *to obtain* or *receive.* Get should not be used in the sense of *to excite, to interest,* or *to understand.* Say: His guitar playing *fascinates* (not *gets*) me. Say: When you talk about lifestyles, I just don't *understand* (not *get*) you.

GOOD, WELL. Do not use the adjective *good* in place of the adverb *well* in structures like the following: John works *well* (not *good*) in the kitchen. Jim Palmer pitched *well* (not *good*) in last night's game.

GRADUATE. One *graduates from,* or *is graduated from,* a school. One does not *graduate a school.* (The student *graduated* [or *was graduated*] from high school.)

HAD OF. Avoid using this to mean *had.* Say: My father always said that he wished he *had* (not *had of*) gone to college.

HANGED, HUNG. When a person is *executed,* he is *hanged.* When anything is *suspended* in space, it is *hung.*

HARDLY. See **CAN'T HARDLY.**

HEALTHFUL, HEALTHY. *Healthful* applies to *conditions that promote health. Healthy* applies to *a state of health.* Say: Stevenson found the climate of Saranac Lakes very *healthful.* Say: Mary is a very *healthy* girl.

IF, WHETHER. Use *whether*—not *if*—in structures that follow verbs like *ask, doubt, know, learn, say.* Say: Hank Aaron didn't know *whether* (not *if*) he was going to break Babe Ruth's homerun record.

IMPLY, INFER. The speaker *implies* when he suggests or hints at. (The owner of the store *implied* that the patron stole a box of toothpicks.) The listener *infers* when he draws a conclusion from facts or evidence. (From what you say, I *infer* that I am about to be discharged.)

IN, INTO. *In* is used to express a location, without the involvement of motion. (The sugar is *in* the cupboard.) *Into* is used to express motion from one place to another. (The housekeeper put the sugar *into* the cupboard.)

IN REGARDS TO. This is incorrect. Say *in regard to* or *with regard to.*

INVENT. See **DISCOVER.**

IRREGARDLESS. Do not use *irregardless.* It is incorrect for *regardless.* (You will not be able to go out tonight regardless of the fact that you have done all of your homework.)

ITS, IT'S. *Its* is the possessive of *it; it's* is the contraction for *it is.*

KIND OF, SORT OF. Do not use these expressions as adverbs. Say: Ali was *quite* (not *kind of* or *sort of*) witty in his post-fight interview.

KIND OF A, SORT OF A. Omit the *a.* Say: What *kind of* (not *kind of a* or *sort of a*) game is lacrosse?

LEARN, TEACH. *Learn* means *gaining knowledge. Teach* means *imparting knowledge.* Say: He *taught* (not *learned*) his brother how to swim.

LEAVE, LET. The word *leave* means *to depart.* (I *leave* today for San Francisco.) The word *let* means to allow. *(Let* me take your place.)

LESS, FEWER. See **FEWER, LESS.**

LIABLE, LIKELY. *Liable* means exposed to something unpleasant. (If you speed, you are *liable* to get a summons.) *Likely* means probable, with reference to either a pleasant or unpleasant happening. (It is *likely* to snow tomorrow.)

LOCATE. Do not use *locate* to mean *settle* or *move to.* Say: We will *move to* (not *locate in*) Florida next year.

MIGHT OF, MUST OF. Omit the *of.* We *might have* or *must have.*

MYSELF, HIMSELF, YOURSELF. These pronouns are to be used as intensives. (The chairman *himself* will open the meeting.) Do not use these pronouns when *me, him,* or *you* will serve. Say: We shall be happy if Joe and *you* (not *yourself)* join us for lunch at the Plaza.

NICE. See **TERRIFIC, TERRIBLE.**

NUMBER, AMOUNT. See **AMOUNT, NUMBER.**

OF, HAVE. Do not use *of* for *have* in structures like *could have.*

OFF OF. Omit the *of.* Say: The book fell *off* (not *off of)* the shelf.

POUR, SPILL. When one *pours,* he does it deliberately. (He carefully *poured* the wine into her glass.) When one *spills,* he does it accidentally. (I carelessly *spilled* some wine on her dress.)

PRACTICAL, PRACTICABLE. *Practical* means *fitted for actual work. Practicable* means *feasible* or *possible.* Say: My business partner is a *practical* man. Say: The boss did not consider the plan *practicable* for this coming year.

PRINCIPAL, PRINCIPLE. *Principal* applies to a *chief* or the *chief part* of something. *Principle* applies to a *basic law.* Say: Mr. Jones is the *principal* of the school. Professor White was the *principal* speaker. Honesty is a good *principle* to follow.

REASON IS BECAUSE. Do not use the expression *reason is because*—it is always incorrect. Say the *reason is that.* (The *reason* Jack failed the course *is that* he didn't study.)

REGARDLESS. See **IRREGARDLESS.**

RESPECTFULLY, RESPECTIVELY. *Respectfully* means *with respect* as in the complimentary close of a letter, *respectfully yours. Respectively* means that each item will be considered *in the order given.* Say: This paper is *respectfully* submitted. Say: The hero, the heroine, and the villain will be played by Albert, Joan, and Harry *respectively.*

SAID. Avoid such legalistic uses of *said* as *said letter, said plan, said program* except in legal writing.

SHOULD OF. Do not use to mean *should have.*

SOME. Do not use *some* when you mean *somewhat.* Say: I'm *somewhat* confused (not *some).*

SPILL, POUR. See **POUR, SPILL.**

SUSPICION. Do not use *suspicion* as a verb when you mean *suspect.*

TAKE, BRING. See **BRING, TAKE.**

TEACH, LEARN. See **LEARN, TEACH.**

TERRIFIC, TERRIBLE. Avoid "lazy words." Many people don't want to take the trouble to use the exact word. They will use words like *terrific, swell, great, beautiful,* etc. to describe anything and everything that is favorable. And they will use words like *terrible, awful, lousy, miserable,* etc. for whatever is unfavorable. Use the exact word. Say: We had a *delicious* (not terrific) meal. Say: We had a *boring* (not *terrible*) *weekend.*

THIS KIND, THESE KIND. *This kind* is correct—as is *that kind, these kinds,* and *those kinds.* (My little brother likes *this kind* of pears.) *These kind* and *those kind* are incorrect.

TRY AND. Do not say *try and.* Say *try to. (Try to* visit me while I am in Florida.)

UNINTERESTED. See **DISINTERESTED.**

WAIT FOR, WAIT ON. *Wait for* means *to await; wait on* means *to serve.* Say: I am waiting *for* (not *on*) Carter to call me on the telephone.

WAY, WAYS. Do not use *ways* for *way.* Say: It is a long *way* (not *ways)* to Japan.

WHERE. Do not use *where* in place of *that* in expressions like the following: I see in the newspaper *that* (not *where)* a nuclear reactor may be built a mile away from our house.

WOULD OF. Do not use to mean *would have.*

Diction, Style, and Sentence Structure

Have your child answer the following questions. Go over his or her answers and compare them with the answers given after the questions. Then show your child how to correct his or her mistakes. You may want to explain to your child the directions to the questions.

Directions: In the exercise below, each sentence is partly or wholly underlined. In some cases, what is underlined is correct; in other cases, it is incorrect. The five choices that follow each sentence represent various ways of writing the underlined part. Choice A is the same as the original underlining, but Choices B, C, D, and E are different. If, in your judgment, the original sentence is better than any of the changed sentences, select Choice A. If another choice produces the only correct sentence, select that choice.

In making your selections, you should observe the rules of standard written English. Your choice must fulfill the requirements of correct grammar, diction (word choice), sentence structure, and style.

If a choice changes the meaning of the original sentence, do not make that choice.

EXAMPLES

1 He likes to sit in the plaza at the base of the monument, listen to the variety of languages being spoken, and eavesdrop on conversation tidbits.

(A) He likes to sit in the plaza at the base of the monument, listen to the variety of languages being spoken, and eavesdrop on conversation tidbits.

(B) He likes to sit in the plaza at the base of the monument, listening to the variety of languages being spoken, and eavesdrop on conversation tidbits.

(C) Sitting in the plaza at the base of the monument, listening to the variety of languages being spoken, and eavesdropping on conversation tidbits are his favorites.

(D) He likes to sit in the plaza at the base of the monument, listen to the variety of languages being spoken, while eavesdropping on conversation tidbits.

(E) As he eavesdrops on conversation tidbits and listens to the kinds of languages being spoken, he likes to sit in the plaza at the base of the monument.

Choice A is correct. Choices B and D are incorrect because they alter the parallel structure of the sentence. Choice C is incorrect because the word <u>favorites</u> is too vague. Choice E is incorrect because the focus of the sentence and the order of activities are changed by the use of the subordinating conjunction <u>as.</u>

2 <u>The approximate number of 6 percent of all those executives who work in major corporations lose their jobs each year.</u>

  (A) The approximate number of 6 percent of all those executives who work in major corporations lose their jobs each year.

  (B) The number of executives working who lose their jobs each year in major corporations approaches 6 percent.

  (C) About 6 percent of all executives in major corporations lose their jobs each year.

  (D) Major corporations executives who lose their jobs each year total approximately 6 percent of all of them.

  (E) About 6 percent of executives lose their jobs each year if they work in major corporations.

Choice A is incorrect because it is wordy. Choice B is incorrect because it contains a misplaced modifier, <u>in major corporations,</u> and is thus unclear. Choice C is correct. Choice D is incorrect because it is wordy and indirect. Choice E is incorrect because it changes the original meaning of the sentence.

3 Some people call the 1970s an era <u>preoccupied with the past</u> because of the revival of interest in the tunes and themes of former years.

  (A) preoccupied with the past

  (B) of past preoccupation

  (C) devoted to unearthing a history of past eras

  (D) of spending time on the past

  (E) absorbed in the past

Choice A is correct. Choice B is incorrect because it is vague. Choice C is incorrect because it is too wordy. Choice D is incorrect because it is awkward. Choice E is incorrect because <u>absorbed</u> is an inappropriate word choice. The rest of the sentence does not bear out the claim of absorption.

4 Block associations in the nation's cities have multiplied recently, <u>activities range</u> from volunteer crime patrols to street festivals.

    (A) activities range

    (B) although activities range

    (C) activities which range

    (D) with activities ranging

    (E) they sponsor activities ranging

Choices A and E are incorrect because they create run-on sentences. Choice B is incorrect because it contains an inappropriate subordinating conjunction, <u>although,</u> which makes the activities seem to be a drawback rather than a positive achievement. Choice C is incorrect because in the clause after the comma, the word <u>activities</u> is left hanging. Choice D is correct.

5 For many people the present is uninviting <u>although</u> the future is uncertain.

    (A) although

    (B) and they also believe that

    (C) which makes it likely that

    (D) therefore

    (E) and

Choice A contains an incorrect use of the subordinating conjunction <u>although</u> because the second clause does not have a conditional relationship to the first clause. It is independent of the first clause. Choice B is incorrect because it is wordy. Choice C is incorrect because it states a conclusion in the second clause that has no basis. Choice D is incorrect because it creates a run-on sentence. Choice E is correct.

Now have your child answer the questions below. Check your child's answers with those given in the book to see whether he or she has approached them correctly.

Directions: Each sentence is partly or wholly underlined. In some cases, what is underlined is correct; in other cases, it is incorrect. The five choices that follow each sentence represent various ways of writing the underlined part. Choice A is the same as the original underlining, but Choices B, C, D, and E are different. If, in your judgment, the original sentence is better than any of the changed sentences, select Choice A. If another choice produces the only correct sentence, select that choice.

In making your selections, you should observe the rules of standard written English. Your choices must fulfill the requirements of correct grammar, diction (word choice), sentence structure, and style.

If a choice changes the meaning of the original sentence, do not make that choice.

QUESTIONS

1 The police chief refused to say <u>about what he would speak</u> at next week's news conference.

   (A) about what he would speak

   (B) the topic of his talk

   (C) what he would discuss

   (D) his topic of conversation

   (E) the subject of his speech

2 Because of a lack of space, speech teachers must <u>work with students sitting in the hallways.</u>

   (A) work with students sitting in the hallways

   (B) work with students as they sit in the hallways

   (C) work with students while sitting in the hallways

   (D) work in the hallways while sitting with students

   (E) sit in the hallways while working with students

3 The chairman postponed the meeting for another week, hoping that emotions <u>would have time to settle in the interim.</u>

   (A) would have time to settle in the interim

   (B) would in the interim have time to settle

   (C) having time would settle in the interim

   (D) in the interim would have time to settle

   (E) would settle in the interim having time

4 The day of dependence on robots to take over household chores is still far in the future.

    (A) of dependence on robots

    (B) of robot dependence

    (C) when it may be possible for reliance on robots

    (D) which is likely for depending on robots

    (E) when you can depend on robots

5 More than performing routine tasks herself, Marion also supervised other workers.

    (A) More than

    (B) Besides

    (C) As an addition to

    (D) Although

    (E) Since

ANSWERS

1 (C) Choices A, B, D, and E are incorrect because they are inappropriate and awkward phrases following the infinitive to say. Choice C is correct.

2 (E) Choices A, B, and C are incorrect because it is not clear whether students or teachers are sitting in the hallways. Choice D is incorrect because its structure makes the meaning of the sentence unclear. Choice E is correct because the role of teachers is made clear by the proper arrangement of clauses.

3 (A) Choice A is correct. Choices B and D are incorrect because the phrase in the interim is misplaced. It should follow the infinitive to settle. Choices C and E are incorrect because of the awkward use of the participle having.

4 (E) Choice A is incorrect because it is too indefinite. Choice B is incorrect because it changes the meaning of the original sentence by using the noun robot as an adjective modifying dependence. Choices C and D are incorrect because they are wordy and indefinite. Choice E is correct.

5 (B) Choices A and C are incorrect because they are inappropriate phrases. Choice B is correct. Choices D and E are incorrect because they change the meaning of the introductory gerund phrase, and thus make the main clause seem illogical.

Logic and Organization

Have your child answer the following questions. Go over his or her answers and compare them with the answers given after the questions. Then show your child how to correct his or her mistakes. You may want to explain to your child the directions to the questions.

Directions: A paragraph, with superscript numerals to indicate the order of each sentence in the paragraph is presented below. You are to answer the questions that follow the paragraph. There are several such paragraphs and question sets in this part of the test.

[1] I know plenty of pet owners who suffer frustration every spring from fleas. [2] It is infuriating to be beaten by enemies so tiny, but in this eternal war the humans are often the losers. [3] Even our most powerful weapons can either prove ineffective or backfire, hurting the animals we try to protect. [4] Many people do not realize how harmful they can be. [5] They can kill baby kittens or even puppies by causing anemia, they can strip an animal of its hair, and they make life unbearable for infested animals, particularly those allergic to their bites. [6] Kittens and puppies under two months can get sick or die if treated with a flea dust or spray, or by nursing from a mother exposed to any kind of flea repellent, including collars. [7] Long-haired cats can't wear flea collars, because they usually develop severe irritations around their necks. [8] A surprising number of animals are allergic to flea deterrents. [9] One of the big problems with flea control is that the control can be more dangerous than the fleas.

EXAMPLE

1 In sentence 2, <u>but</u> should be

   (A) left as it is

   (B) changed to <u>so</u>

   (C) omitted

   (D) changed to <u>and</u>

   (E) changed to <u>but often</u>

Choice A is correct. The conjunction <u>but</u> is correctly used to introduce a fact that is the opposite of what one would want. Choice B is incorrect because <u>so</u> would mean that a conclusion follows, which is not the case in this sentence. Choice C is incorrect because leaving out <u>but</u> would result in a run-on sentence, clearly lacking a joining word like <u>but</u>. Choice D is incorrect because the sentence would lack the ironic force of showing that a human being can be out-classed by a flea. Choice E is incorrect because of the unnecessary repetition of the adverb <u>often</u>.

2 Sentence 9 should be

    (A) left as it is

    (B) placed after sentence 5

    (C) omitted

    (D) placed after sentence 7

    (E) joined to sentence 8 with <u>and</u>

Choice A is incorrect because sentence 9 contains a general idea that should clearly precede sentences 6, 7, and 8. Choice B is the correct placement for sentence 9, which is a broad statement and should appear before the examples listed in sentences 6, 7, and 8. Choice C is incorrect because the idea in sentence 9 is necessary as a bridge between sentences 4 and 5, which talk about the dangerous nature of fleas, and sentences 6, 7, and 8, which deal with the effects of flea control on dogs and cats. Choice D is incorrect because placing sentence 9 here would destroy the logical nature of the selection since the idea, expressed in sentence 9 has already been elaborated on in sentences 6 and 7. Choice E is incorrect because sentence 9 clearly introduces the ideas in sentences 6, 7, and 8. It could not serve as the second half of a concluding sentence.

3 In sentence 7, <u>usually</u> should be

    (A) left as it is

    (B) changed to <u>infrequently</u>

    (C) changed to <u>every once in a while</u>

    (D) placed at the end of the sentence, after the word <u>necks</u>

    (E) changed to <u>most usually</u>

Choice A is correct. Choice B is incorrect because <u>infrequently</u> means <u>seldom</u>, which is not the meaning of the sentence. Choice C is incorrect because it, too, is opposite in meaning to the idea of the sentence. It is also an awkward phrase as used in this sentence. Choice D is incorrect because the adverb <u>usually</u> should be placed as close as possible to the word it describes, which is develop. Otherwise, the meaning is not clear. Choice E is incorrect because there is no comparison in the sentence and therefore no need to use the form most usually.

4 In sentence 4, they should be

    (A) left as it is

    (B) changed to people

    (C) changed to weapons

    (D) changed to fleas

    (E) changed to animals

Choice A is incorrect because the pronoun they is unclear regarding the word it represents. It could refer to people, weapons, animals, or fleas. Choices B, C, and E are incorrect because the intention of the passage is to show that fleas are harmful, not people, weapons, or animals. Choice D is correct and avoids ambiguity (an unclear meaning).

5 Sentence 5 should be

    (A) made into two sentences by placing a period after hair

    (B) changed by placing the conjunction and before the second clause, which would then begin "and they can strip an animal. . . ."

    (C) shortened by eliminating the last section beginning with particularly

    (D) changed by adding the words which are after the pronoun those in the last part

    (E) left as it is

Choice E is correct. Choice A is incorrect because placing a period after hair would transform the first two clauses into a run-on sentence. Choice B is incorrect because adding and ruins the rhythm of the original sentence. Whenever a series of words, phrases, or clauses is used, the conjunction is usually placed only before the last item or section of the series, not before each part of the series. Choice C is incorrect because leaving out the last phrase would omit a piece of information that is important in understanding the damaging effect that fleas can have on animals that are allergic to their bite. Choice D is incorrect because adding the words which are after the word those is unnecessary.

Now have your child answer the questions below. Check your child's answers with those given in the book to see whether he or she has approached them correctly.

Directions: A paragraph, with superscript numerals to indicate the order of each sentence in the paragraph, is presented below. You are to answer the questions that follow the paragraph. There are several such paragraphs and question sets in this part of the test.

[1] Most doctors across the country are probably not yet questioning patients about what kind of light they live under every day, some doctors are coming to believe that this query may be an entirely relevant one. [2] Unfortunately, the artificial light most of us live under is vastly inferior to the natural variety, so the theory goes, and we may be as starved for certain constituents of full-spectrum light as we are for the nutrients and vitamins taken out of refined foods. [3] Light, they contend, is a nutrient just as much as water or food, and is absorbed by our bodies and used in a variety of metabolic processes. [4] Studies done in schools around the country showed that children who spent a year in classrooms that had full-spectrum rather than cool-white fluorescent light were less hyperactive, had better grades, and grew faster. [5] In another study it was found that children who spent their days under cool-white light developed significantly more cavities than those working under light that had low levels of ultraviolet added to it. [6] Zoos have been finding that pit vipers, which have long preferred to starve rather than eat in captivity, were accepting food within a few number of days after sunlight-simulating lamps containing ultraviolet were installed.

QUESTIONS

1 Sentence 1 would be correct if it were to begin with

(A) Because

(B) In general

(C) Considering

(D) Though

(E) It is safe to say that

2 Sentence 3 is best placed

(A) at the beginning of the passage

(B) after sentence 1

(C) where it is now

(D) after sentence 4

(E) after sentence 5

3 Were the passage to be divided into three paragraphs, the second paragraph should begin with

(A) sentence 2

(B) sentence 3

(C) sentence 4

(D) sentence 5

(E) sentence 6

4 In sentence 6 the phrase <u>within a few number of days</u> should

(A) remain the same

(B) have <u>within</u> changed to <u>after</u>

(C) be reduced to <u>a few days</u>

(D) be replaced by <u>shortly</u>

(E) be replaced by <u>not long</u>

ANSWERS

1 (D) Choices A and C are incorrect because they imply a cause/effect relationship not indicated by the remainder of the sentence. Choices B and E create run-on sentences. Choice D is correct because it establishes the correct relationship in both structure and meaning.

2 (B) Choice A leaves the meaning of the sentence unclear because there is no preceding noun to which <u>they</u> can refer. Choice B is correct because <u>they</u> clearly refers to the doctors who think sunlight is important for health, and because the sentence provides a transition to sentence 2. Choice C is incorrect because the referent of <u>they</u> is unclear. Choice D is incorrect because the logical flow from sentence 4 to sentence 5 is interrupted. Choice E is incorrect because grammatically <u>they</u> would refer to <u>children</u> in sentence 5; the meaning of the sentences, however, makes this reference impossible.

3 (C) Choices A and B are incorrect because sentences 2 and 3 are part of the general introduction. Choice C is correct because sentence 4 is the beginning of a separate topic giving specific information about how some artificial light is harmful. Choice D is incorrect because sentence 5 gives information similar to that of sentence 5 and therefore belongs in the same paragraph. Choice E is incorrect because sentence 6 is the second break in the passage; consequently, it could be the beginning of the third paragraph.

4 (C) Choice A is incorrect because a few number of days is needlessly wordy. Choice B is incorrect because the phrase still remains unwieldy. Choice C is correct because the meaning is conveyed clearly and concisely. Choices D and E are incorrect because they are too vague: They could refer to several minutes, several hours, or several days.

MATH STRATEGIES

A Note to Parents

You and your child will be presented with various strategies and critical-thinking skills to be used in solving math problems. If as you go along you begin to feel that your child is lacking certain basic information in an area of math, such as geometry, refer to the section entitled "Math Words, Concepts and Rules Your Child Should Know," on pages 156–172. Your child can also look at "Math Shortcuts Your Child Should Know," on pages 173–182. Finally, if you feel that your child should brush up on his or her basics *before* beginning to learn the strategies, have a look at "The Thirty-Two Key Basic Math Problems for Grades 6 • 7 • 8 • 9," on pages 183–184. You may want to have your child work on them before teaching your child the beginning strategic material.

Before beginning to work on the math strategies presented in this part of the book, you should also review the four-step learning method described in the "Introduction to Parents," on page 16.

BASIC MATH STRATEGIES

The math strategies presented below will help your child to answer math questions more quickly and accurately by enabling your child to: first, focus his or her mind on each problem in the most appropriate way, and second, use a variety of strategic shortcuts in working out the solutions to problems.

MATH STRATEGY 1:
Know How to Approach Solutions to Math Questions

One of the most important things to know in answering any math question is how to *start* the solution. So many students rush into a solution without taking the time to think about what the question is really asking or aiming at.

The key to solving math questions is knowing *how to extract from the question the useful pieces of information* that will enable your child to solve it. Here are some examples:

EXAMPLE 1

Paul earns $22 in 5 days. How much does Paul earn in 8 days if he works at the same rate of pay?

(A) $88.00 (B) $40.00 (C) $35.20 (D) $35.40

Don't just rush into the problem by multiplying the numbers given. Think about what piece or pieces of information can be extracted from this question that will be useful in finding a solution. If Paul earns $22 in 5 days, you can find out how much money he earns in 1 day. Just divide 22 by 5:

$$\frac{22}{5} = 4.40$$

So Paul earns $4.40 in 1 day. Now you've got something very useful. If you want to find how much he earns in 8 days, just multiply $4.40 by 8:

$$\begin{array}{r} 4.40 \\ \times\ \ \ 8 \\ \hline 35.20 \end{array}$$

Choice C is correct.

Let's look at another problem that has some piece of information that will start you off in the right direction toward solving the problem.

EXAMPLE 2

The number of pencils in 7 boxes, each containing 30 pencils, is the same number of pencils in

(A) 5 boxes containing 20 pencils in each box
(B) 10 boxes containing 15 pencils in each box
(C) 15 boxes containing 20 pencils in each box
(D) 21 boxes containing 10 pencils in each box

How do we approach this question? What do we look for first? Let's look at the choices. They all state the number of boxes and how many pencils there are in each box. This gives us the *total number* of pencils in all the boxes for each choice. The question tells us the number of boxes and how many pencils there are in each box. This also gives us the *total number* of pencils. So we can find this total number by multiplying 7 by 30. This number is 210.

Now let's look for a choice whose numbers (boxes × pencils) give you 210. Choice D has 21 boxes with 10 pencils (21 × 10 = 210). So Choice D is correct.

EXAMPLE 3

In the figure below, you are given a 6-minute clock. The clock starts at 0 and stops 243 minutes later. At which number does the clock stop?

(A) 1 (B) 2 (C) 3 (D) 4

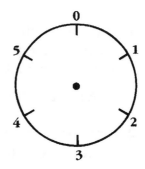

How do we approach a problem like this? We have to think that the clock will reach the 0-minute mark again in 6 minutes, again in 12 minutes, again in 18, and so on. In other words, it will reach the 0 mark in every *multiple of 6 minutes.* So let's find out how many 6's go into the total time of 243 minutes: This will tell us how many times it hit the 0 mark and what was left over.

$$
\begin{array}{r}
40 \text{ remainder } 3 \\
6\overline{)243} \\
24 \\
\overline{03} \\
0 \\
\overline{3}
\end{array}
$$

The clock hit the 0 digit 40 times and moved another 3 digits. So it ended up on the digit 3. Choice C is correct.

After you have shown your child the previous three problems with solutions, have him or her try the problems below and check to see whether he or she used the strategy explained in the solutions that follow the problems.

PROBLEMS

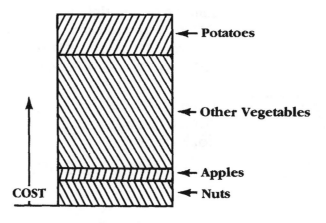

1 The bar graph above describes the cost of various items used in a particular recipe. What item costs approximately 60 percent of the total cost for all the items?

   (A) nuts (B) apples (C) potatoes (D) other vegetables

2 How many teachers teach at a high school if the ratio of teachers to students in that school is 1 to 5 and there are 200 students in the school?

   (A) 4 (B) 40 (C) 400 (D) 1,000

3 The dues for a certain club are $5 per month. How much would a person save in one year if he or she paid $50 for a yearly subscription to the club and did not have to pay dues for the year?

   (A) $60 (B) $50 (C) $30 (D) $10

$\pi = 3.14$
Constant

4 A lemon syrup calls for 2 ounces of lemon juice to every 12 ounces of plain syrup . To make 42 ounces of lemon syrup, how many ounces of plain syrup must be used?

(A) 14 (B) 16 (C) 36 (D) 2

5 The radius of Circle A is 10 and the radius of Circle B is 5. How much greater is the area of Circle A than the area of Circle B?

(A) 25π (B) 50π (C) 75π (D) 100π

Area of circle
$= \pi r^2$
Circ. of circle
$= \pi d \sim$ diameter
$= 2\pi r$

SOLUTIONS

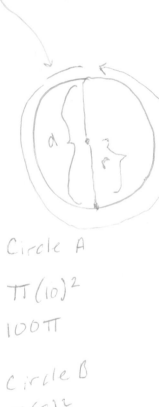

Circle A
$\pi (10)^2$
$= 100\pi$

Circle B
$\pi (5)^2$
$= 25\pi$

1 (D) What you want to know is what section of the graph looks as if it is 60% of the total graph (total cost). You can see that "Other Vegetables" make up a block that is about three fifths, or 60% of the total. All of the other sections make up less than one half (50 percent) of the total.

2 (B) You want to find the number of teachers in the school. You are told that the ratio of teachers to students is 1 to 5 and there are 200 students. First use the fact that the ratio is 1 to 5.

$$\frac{1}{5} = \frac{\text{number of teachers}}{\text{number of students}}$$

Now you use the fact that there are 200 students in the school. We get:

$$\frac{1}{5} = \frac{\text{number of teachers}}{200}$$

Multiply both sides of the above equation by 200 to get rid of the 200 in the denominator of the right side of the equation:

$$\frac{1}{5} \times 200 = \frac{\text{number of teachers}}{200} \times 200$$

$$40 = \text{number of teachers}$$

3 (D) You are told that the dues for each month are $5. You are looking for how much you will save in one year. So let's find out how much it will cost per year at $5 per month. Just multiply $5 by 12 since there are 12 months in a year ($5 × 12 = $60 per year). If you pay $50 on a subscription, you save $10 ($60 − $50 = $10).

4 (C) You are told that 2 ounces of lemon juice are used with 12 ounces of plain syrup. You want to find what you must use to make 42 ounces of lemon syrup. You must mix a certain amount of lemon juice with a certain amount of plain syrup to get a total amount of 42 ounces of lemon syrup. How do you approach this question? Try to figure out something from the information you are given. You know that 2 ounces of lemon juice are mixed with 12 ounces of plain syrup to make lemon syrup. Since 2 + 12 = 14, the 2 ounces of lemon juice + 12 ounces of plain syrup make 14 ounces of lemon syrup. You want 42 ounces of lemon syrup. To get 42 ounces, you will need <u>3</u> times as much of each ingredient, since 14 × <u>3</u> = 42. So instead of 12 ounces of plain syrup, which would make 14 ounces of lemon syrup, you will need 36 ounces (12 × <u>3</u> = 36) of plain syrup to make 42 ounces (14 × <u>3</u> = 42) of lemon syrup.

5 (C) You are told that the radius of Circle A is 10 and the radius of Circle B is 5. You want to know the difference between the <u>areas</u>. So what you have to think about is how to relate <u>area</u> to <u>radius</u>.

First find the areas of Circle A and Circle B:

area of Circle A = π × radius of Circle A   × radius of Circle A
area of Circle B = π × radius of Circle B   × radius of Circle B

We know that the radius of Circle A is 10 and the radius of Circle B is 5, so

area of Circle A = π × 10 × 10 = 100π
area of Circle B = π × 5 × 5 = 25π

The difference in areas is just

area of Circle A − area of Circle B

The difference is 100π − 25π = 75π.

MATH STRATEGY 2:
Use Math Symbols for Words

Math problems expressed in nonmathematical terms are the most difficult kinds of math questions. If your child does not know the right strategy, he or she could become exhausted trying to do some of these brain-racking problems. However, there is a strategy that can make these problems much simpler: substituting math symbols for words.

As early as possible, you should familiarize your child with math symbols, so that he or she can use them as a shortcut in solving those kinds of problems that are expressed mostly in words. Here's an example:

EXAMPLE 1:

12 is what percent of 6?

(A) 72 (B) 2 (C) 20 (D) 200

Here's how to do the problem using the verbal-math translation method:

Translate:

$$\frac{\text{is}}{\text{what}} \quad \frac{\text{to} \ =}{\text{to} \ x \ (\text{the unknown})}$$
$$\frac{\text{percent}}{\text{of}} \quad \frac{\text{to} \ /100}{\text{to} \ \times \ (\text{times})}$$

So the problem becomes:

$$
\begin{array}{cccccc}
12 & \text{is} & \text{what} & \text{percent} & \text{of} & 6 \\
\downarrow & \downarrow & \downarrow & \downarrow & \downarrow & \downarrow \\
12 & = & x & /100 & \times & 6
\end{array}
$$

That is, $12 = \dfrac{x}{100} \times 6$

Divide both sides of the equation by 6:

$$\frac{12}{6} = \frac{x}{100} \times \frac{6}{6}$$

$$2 = \frac{x}{100}$$

$$200 = x$$

Choice D is correct.

The table below will help your child in changing words into math symbols. Your child should gradually become familiar with this table.

Word	Equivalent Math Symbol	Word	Equivalent Math Symbol
and	+	of	×
added to	+	twice as many	2 ×
gave	+	half as many	½ ×
got	+	percent	$\overline{100}$
gained	+	increased 20 percent	$+ \frac{20}{100} \times$ original value
greater than	+		
has, had	+	reduced 20 percent	$- \frac{20}{100} \times$ original value
increased by	+		
received	+	are, is, was	=
sum of	+	equal to	=
m years from now	+ m	has, had	=
decreased by	−	same as	=
difference of	−	less than	<
less	−	shorter than	<
lost	−	younger than	<
owe	−	greater than	>
subtract from	−	older than	>
m years ago	− m	taller than	>
		John, Phil, Sam, etc.	J, P, S, etc.
		what	? or □
		what (or any unknown)	x, n, N, etc.

Note: If $a > b$, and $b > c$, then $a > c$.
  $a > b$ is the same as $b < a$.
  $b > c$ is the same as $c < b$.
  $a > c$ is the same as $c < a$.

Let's try two more examples using the above table.

EXAMPLE 2

If a sweater originally cost $21.50 and is reduced 40%, by how much was the sweater reduced?

(A) $12.90 (B) $8.60 (C) $21.40 (D) $4.50

Use the translation method:

Original cost

21.50 reduced 40%
↓   ↓   ↓

$$21.50 \quad - \quad \frac{40}{100} \, (21.50)$$

Reduced by

$$\frac{40}{100} \times 21.50 = 8.60$$

Thus Choice B is correct.

EXAMPLE 3

Mary is taller than John. Paul is shorter than John. Describe the heights of Mary, John, and Paul from tallest to shortest:

(A) Mary, John, Paul
(B) Paul, John, Mary
(C) John, Paul, Mary
(D) John, Mary, Paul

Translate from words to math:

Let Mary be M
John be J
Paul be P

Translate:

Mary is taller than John

$$M \qquad > \qquad J$$

Paul is shorter than John
$$P \qquad < \qquad J$$

Since $M > J$ and $P < J$ ($J > P$ is the same as $P < J$) then $M > J$ and $J > P$. And if you look at the translation table above, you'll see that since $M > J$ and $J > P$, $M > P$. So $M > J > P$.
Choice A is correct.

Now have your child try these examples. Go over the solutions with your child, making sure he or she approaches the questions with the correct strategy.

PROBLEMS

1 A television usually priced at $160 is reduced 20 percent. What is the new price?

   (A) $128 (B) $145 (C) $132 (D) $32

The following two questions refer to the graph below:

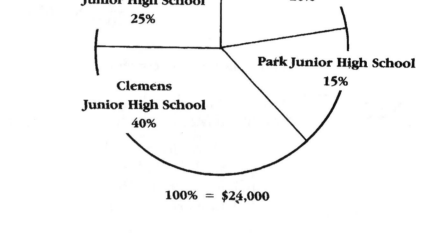

School Contributions to County Christmas Fund

Lincoln Junior High School 20%

Washington Junior High School 25%

Park Junior High School 15%

Clemens Junior High School 40%

100% = $24,000

2 The contribution from Washington Junior High School was what part of the contributions from the other schools?

   (A) $\frac{1}{2}$ (B) $\frac{1}{3}$ (C) $\frac{1}{4}$ (D) $\frac{1}{5}$

3 What contribution did Lincoln Junior High School make?

   (A) $24,000 (B) $12,000 (C) $6,400 (D) $4,800

4 There are 24 girls at a party. The ratio of boys to girls at the party is 3 to 4. How many boys are there at the party?

   (A) 12 (B) 18 (C) 28 (D) 36

5 15 is what percent of 45?

   (A) 20 (B) 33⅓ (C) 45 (D) 50

6 25 is 150 percent of what number?

   (A) 8 (B) 8⅓ (C) 16⅔ (D) 80

7 Harry's father gives Harry $2 for every log over 10 that Harry brings into the house. If Harry brings L logs into the house where L is greater than 10, how many dollars does Harry make?

(A) $2L$ (B) $(L - 10)2$ (C) $(10 - L)2$ (D) $(L + 10)2$

SOLUTIONS

1 (A) Translate words into math:

$$160 - \frac{20}{100} \times 160 = \text{new price}$$

usual price   price reduced 20%

$$160 - \frac{20 \times 160}{100} = \text{new price}$$

Reduce: $$160 - \frac{2\emptyset \times 16\emptyset}{1\emptyset\emptyset} = \text{new price}$$

$$160 - 32 = \text{new price}$$

$$128 = \text{new price}$$

2 (B) Translate words into math:

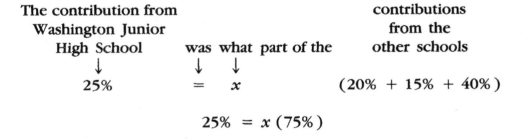

The contribution from Washington Junior High School was what part of the contributions from the other schools

25% = x (20% + 15% + 40%)

$$25\% = x\,(75\%)$$

Divide both sides by 75 to get x alone:

$$\frac{25}{75} = x$$

Reducing:

$$\frac{1}{3} = x$$

3 (D) Translate words into math:

Lincoln Junior High School made 20% of total. 100% = $24,000
(given)

$$20\% \quad \text{of} \quad \text{total} \quad =$$
$$\downarrow \qquad \downarrow \qquad \downarrow$$
$$\frac{20}{100} \times 24{,}000 = \frac{480{,}000}{100}$$

$$= \quad 4800$$

4 (B) translate words into math:

Call the number of boys b. Now translate:
The ratio of boys to girls is 3 to 4: Note: 24 girls (given)

$$\frac{b}{24} = \frac{3}{4}$$

Multiply by 24 to get b alone:

$$\frac{b}{24} \times 24 = \frac{3}{4} \times 24$$

$$b = \frac{3}{4} \times 24$$

Reduce:

$$b = \frac{3}{\cancel{4}} \times \cancel{24}^{6}$$

$$b = 3 \times 6 = 18$$

Something you may want to note: Since it was stated that the ratio of boys to girls was 3 to 4, there must be fewer boys than girls. So there must be *less than 24* boys because there are 24 girls. You can therefore rule out Choices C and D immediately.

5 (B) Translate:

$$15 \quad \text{is} \quad \text{what} \quad \text{percent} \quad \text{of} \quad 45$$
$$\downarrow \quad \downarrow \quad \downarrow \qquad \downarrow \qquad \downarrow \quad \downarrow$$
$$15 \quad = \quad x \qquad \frac{}{100} \quad \times \quad 45$$

$$15 = \left(\frac{x}{100}\right) \times 45$$

Divide by 45:

$$\frac{15}{45} = \frac{x}{100}$$

Multiply by 100:

$$\frac{15}{45} \times 100 = x$$

Reduce:

$$\frac{1}{3} \times 100 = x$$

$$33\frac{1}{3} = x$$

6 (C) Translate:

25 is 150 percent of what number?
↓ ↓ ↓   ↓   ↓   ↓
25 = 150 $\dfrac{}{100}$ × x

$$25 = \frac{150}{100}\, x$$

Multiply by 100:

$$25 \times 100 = 150x$$

Divide by 150:

$$\frac{25 \times 100}{150} = x$$

Reduce:

$$\frac{\overset{5}{\cancel{25}} \times 10\cancel{0}}{\underset{3}{\cancel{150}}} = \frac{50}{3} = 16\frac{2}{3}$$

7 (B) Translate:

L is the number of logs Harry brings into the house.
He gets \$2 for each log (over 10).
So $L - 10$ is the number of logs he gets paid for.
You can try an example to see if you're right:
Suppose he carries 11 logs into the house. He gets paid for $L - 10 = 11 - 10 = 1$ log, which seems right.
Since he gets paid \$2 for each log over 10, $(L - 10) \times 2$ must be the amount of dollars he makes.

MATH STRATEGY 3:
Know When and How to Approximate

Many times your child will encounter a question that asks not for an exact answer but for an *approximation* to an answer. At other times your child may want to approximate to find an answer more rapidly. So it is important to know how and when to approximate. The following examples show typical problems where this strategy should be used.

EXAMPLE 1

The length of a fence is 32.96 meters. One fourth the length of the fence would be approximately how many meters?

(A) 7 (B) 8 (C) 9 (D) 10

Whenever you want to approximate an answer, always look at the answer choices just to see how far your approximation should go. In the question above, you can see that all of the answer choices are *whole numbers*. So let's approximate 32.96 by the *closest whole number* 33. Now you'd like to take one fourth of 33. Take one fourth of 32—it's easier. One fourth of 32 is 8. Choice B is correct.

EXAMPLE 2

15 is closest to which other number?

(A) $15 - \dfrac{1}{100}$ (B) $15 + \dfrac{15}{100}$ (C) $15 \times \dfrac{1}{100}$ (D) $15 \div \dfrac{1}{100}$

Looking at the choices, you can see that multiplying and dividing by 1/100 (Choices C and D) changes the number 15 very much. Subtracting only 1/100 from 15 does not change 15 as much as adding 15/100 to 15. So Choice A must be correct.

EXAMPLE 3

$\sqrt{24}$ is closest to (A) 3.9 (B) 4.9 (C) 5.9 (D) 6.9

$\sqrt{24}$ means that the number when multiplied by itself gives you 24. So which of the choices when multiplied by itself gives you a number closest to 24. Approximate all of the choices:

(A) 3.9—4
(B) 4.9—5
(C) 5.9—6
(D) 6.9—7

You can see that Choice B is closest since $5 \times 5 = 25$, which is very close to 24.

EXAMPLE 4

7,876 rounded to the nearest hundred is

(A) 7,800 (B) 7,870 (C) 7,880 (D) 7,900

Here you have to read the question carefully. It says you want to find 7,876 rounded to the nearest hundred. That means the number you are looking for must end in 00. So, although 7,880 (Choice C) is closest to 7,876, it is not rounded to the nearest hundred. The number to the nearest hundred is 7,900 (Choice D).

EXAMPLE 5

19 × 48 is closest to

(A) 900 (B) 1,000 (C) 1,100 (D) 1,200

Look at the choices. They all end in 00. So let's approximate 19 by 20 and 48 by 50. Now multiply 20 × 50 = 1,000. Choice B is correct.

EXAMPLE 6

$\dfrac{397}{2,401}$ is closest to

(A) $\dfrac{1}{6}$ (B) $\dfrac{1}{8}$ (C) $\dfrac{1}{4}$ (D) $\dfrac{1}{60}$

Approximate 397 as 400 and 2,401 as 2,400. So you want to get $\dfrac{400}{2,400}$. Reduce and cancel: $\dfrac{4\cancel{00}}{2,4\cancel{00}} = \dfrac{1}{6}$. Choice A is correct.

Have your child work on these questions. Go over his or her answers to see whether your child has approached the problems correctly by referring to the appropriate strategic explanations.

PROBLEMS

1 7.3 × .4 × .09 =
   (A) 26.28
   (B) 2.628
   (C) .2628
   (D) .02628

3 .46 × 32 =
   (A) 1.472
   (B) 14.72
   (C) 147.2
   (D) 1472

2 31 + 71 + 98 + 99 is closest to
   (A) 310
   (B) 300
   (C) 290
   (D) 280

4 51,289 − 4,996 is closest to
   (A) 45,000
   (B) 46,000
   (C) 47,000
   (D) 48,000

5 If $x \not\doteq \sqrt{67}$, then which is true?

(A) $8 < x < 9$

(B) $7 < x < 8$

(C) $6 < x < 7$

(D) $5 < x < 6$

SOLUTIONS

1 (C) You can see by looking at the choices that all you need to do is find where the decimal point should be placed. You can approximate very roughly:

$$7.3 \times .4 \times .09$$
$$\downarrow \quad \downarrow \quad \downarrow$$
$$7 \times .4 \times .1$$
$$\underbrace{\qquad} \quad \downarrow$$
$$2.8 \quad \times .1$$
$$\underbrace{\qquad}$$
$$.28$$

Choice C is closest.

2 (B) By looking at the choices, you can approximate:

$$31 + 71 + 98 + 99$$
$$\downarrow \quad \downarrow \quad \downarrow \quad \downarrow$$
$$30 + 70 + 100 + 100$$
$$\underbrace{\qquad} \quad \downarrow \quad \downarrow$$
$$100 \quad + 100 + 100$$
$$\underbrace{\qquad\qquad\qquad}$$
$$300$$

Choice B is correct.

3 (B) Look at the choices. You can see that it is possible to roughly approximate:

$$.46 \times 32$$
$$\downarrow \quad \downarrow \quad \downarrow$$
$$.5 \times 30$$
$$\underbrace{\qquad}$$
$$15$$

Choice B (15) is closest to 14.72.

4 (B) Look at the choices. They all end in 000. So approximate 51,289 by 51,000 and 4,996 by 5,000. Now $51,000 - 5,000 = 46,000$ (Choice B).

5 (A) $\sqrt{67}$ means that the number when multiplied by itself gives you 67. You know that $8 \times 8 = 64$, $9 \times 9 = 81$. So the number that gives you 67, when multiplied by itself, must be between 8 and 9. That is, it must be greater than 8 but less than 9 (Choice A).

MATH STRATEGY 4: Reduce or Simplify Before Calculating

Often a child will go through a series of calculations without realizing that by reducing certain quantities first or simplifying others, he or she can arrive at a solution much more quickly. Here are some examples:

EXAMPLE 1

$\frac{1}{5}$ of (52 hours and 10 minutes) =

(A) 12 hours and 24 minutes
(B) 11 hours and 24 minutes
(C) 11 hours
(D) 10 hours and 26 minutes

<u>Don't</u> add 52 hours and 10 minutes yet.

$\frac{1}{5}$ of (52 hours and 10 minutes) =

$$\frac{52 \text{ hours}}{5} \quad + \quad \frac{10 \text{ minutes}}{5}$$

$$\downarrow \qquad\qquad\qquad \downarrow$$

$$10\frac{2}{5} \text{ hours} \quad + \quad 2 \text{ minutes}$$

$$\downarrow \qquad\qquad\qquad \downarrow$$

$$10 \text{ hours} \quad + \quad 2 \text{ minutes}$$

$$+ \frac{2}{5} \times 60 \text{ minutes}$$

$$\downarrow \qquad\qquad\qquad \downarrow$$

$$10 \text{ hours} \quad + \quad 2 \text{ minutes}$$
$$+ \text{ 24 minutes} \underbrace{\qquad\qquad\qquad}$$

$$10 \text{ hours} \quad + \quad 26 \text{ minutes}$$

Choice D is correct.

EXAMPLE 2

82 + (30% of 50) − (20% of 50) =
(A) 87 (B) 88 (C) 89 (D) 90

Don't calculate 30% of 50 and 20% of 50. Look for a simpler way.
30% of 50 − 20% of 50 = (30% − 20%) of 50

$$= \quad 10\% \text{ of } 50$$

$$= \frac{10}{100} \times 50$$

$$= \quad 5$$

All you have to do now is add 82 to 5 to get 87. Choice A is correct.

EXAMPLE 3

$$\frac{775 \times 3}{15} =$$

(A) 155 (B) 165 (C) 175 (D) 185

Don't multiply 775 × 3 and then divide by 15!
First reduce:

$$\frac{775 \times 3}{15}$$

$$\frac{775 \times \overset{1}{\cancel{3}}}{\underset{5}{\cancel{15}}}$$

$$\begin{array}{c} 155 \\ \dfrac{\cancel{775}}{\underset{1}{\cancel{5}}} \end{array}$$

Choice A is correct.

EXAMPLE 4

$$\frac{3}{4} \times \frac{4}{5} \times \frac{5}{6} \times \frac{6}{7} = \frac{3}{7}$$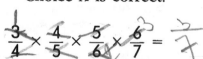

(A) $\frac{21}{78}$ (B) $\frac{36}{85}$ (C) $\frac{179}{235}$ (D) $\frac{3}{7}$

Don't multiply 3 × 4 × 5 × 6 and then divide that by 4 × 5 ×
6 × 7!

Notice that a denominator of one fraction cancels with the numerator of the next fraction:

$$\frac{3}{\cancel{4}} \times \frac{\cancel{4}}{\cancel{5}} \times \frac{\cancel{5}}{\cancel{6}} \times \frac{\cancel{6}}{7} = \frac{3}{7}$$ Choice D is correct.

EXAMPLE 5

If $\dfrac{250}{\square} = \dfrac{25}{3}$ then $\square$ =

(A) 30 (B) 32 (C) 34 (D) 36

Don't divide $\dfrac{25}{3}$!

Get the value of $\square$ by cross-multiplying, but don't multiply out!

$$\frac{250}{\square} \diagdown \frac{25}{3}$$

$$250 \times 3 = \square \times 25$$

Now divide by 25:

$$\frac{250 \times 3}{25} = \square \times \frac{25}{25}$$

Reduce:

$$\frac{\overset{10}{\cancel{250}} \times 3}{\cancel{25}} = \square$$

$$30 = \square$$

Choice A is correct.

Have your child work on these questions, then check to see whether his or her method of approach is the same as the one used in the book for the solutions to these questions.

PROBLEMS

1 $\frac{1}{4}$ of the total of 25 hours and 8 minutes is equal to

(A) 6 hours and 23 minutes
(B) 6 hours and 17 minutes
(C) 8 hours and 15 minutes
(D) 8 hours and 25 minutes

2 $(50 \times 71) - (40 \times 71) =$ $(50-40)(71)$

   (A) 710 (B) 810 (C) 910 (D) 1,010

3 $\dfrac{27 \times 42}{21 \times 36} =$

   (A) $1\dfrac{1}{2}$ (B) $1\dfrac{3}{4}$ (C) $1\dfrac{7}{8}$ (D) $1\dfrac{8}{15}$

4 $1\dfrac{1}{4} \times \dfrac{4}{5} \times 1\dfrac{2}{3} \times \dfrac{3}{5} =$

   (A) $1\dfrac{2}{25}$ (B) $1\dfrac{7}{15}$ (C) 1 (D) none of these

5 $\dfrac{420}{75} = \dfrac{42}{\square} \cdot \square =$

   (A) 7.5 (B) 8.5 (C) 9.5 (D) 10.5

SOLUTIONS

1 (B) *Don't* add 25 hours + 8 minutes yet.

$$\frac{1}{4} \text{ of } 25 \text{ hours} + 8 \text{ minutes} = \frac{25 \text{ hours}}{4} + \frac{8 \text{ minutes}}{4}$$

$$\downarrow \qquad\qquad \downarrow$$

$$6\tfrac{1}{4} \text{ hours} + 2 \text{ minutes}$$

$$\downarrow \qquad\qquad \downarrow$$

$$6 \text{ hrs } 15 \text{ min} + 2 \text{ minutes}$$

$$= 6 \text{ hrs } 17 \text{ min}$$

2 (A) *Don't* multiply 50×71 and 40×71!

$$50 \times 71 - 40 \times 71 = (50 - 40) \times 71$$

$$= 10 \times 71$$

$$= 710$$

3 (A) *Don't* multiply 27×42 and then divide by 21×36!

Reduce:

$$\frac{27 \times \overset{2}{\cancel{42}}}{\cancel{21} \times 36}$$

$$\frac{\overset{3}{\cancel{27}} \times 2}{\underset{4}{\cancel{36}}} = \frac{6}{4} = \frac{3}{2} = 1\frac{1}{2}$$

4   (C) First simplify by getting all fractions to have the same form. Try to get all fractions to be one type, like simple fractions.

$$1\frac{1}{4} = \frac{5}{4} \text{ and } 1\frac{2}{3} = \frac{5}{3}$$

So

$$1\frac{1}{4} \times \frac{4}{5} \times 1\frac{2}{3} \times \frac{3}{5}$$
$$\downarrow \qquad \downarrow \qquad \downarrow \qquad \downarrow$$
$$\frac{5}{4} \times \frac{4}{5} \times \frac{5}{3} \times \frac{3}{5}$$

Cancel numerators and denominators that are the same:
$$\frac{\cancel{5}}{\cancel{4}} \times \frac{\cancel{4}}{\cancel{5}} \times \frac{\cancel{5}}{\cancel{3}} \times \frac{\cancel{3}}{\cancel{5}}$$
$$\downarrow$$
$$1$$

5   (A) *Don't* divide 420 by 75!

Cross-multiply:

$$\frac{420}{75} = \frac{42}{\square}$$

$$420 \times \square = 42 \times 75 \text{ (Don't multiply } 42 \times 75!)$$

Divide by 42:

$$\frac{420 \times \square}{42} = \frac{\cancel{42} \times 75}{\cancel{42}}$$

$$10 \times \square = 75$$

Divide both sides of the equation by 10:

$$\frac{10 \times \square}{10} = \frac{75}{10}$$
$$\downarrow$$
$$\square = 7.5$$

MATH STRATEGY 5:
Start with Last Choice When Testing Choices

The test designer is a very clever person. The test maker expects that if your child has to try all the choices to see which one is correct, your child will start with Choice A. In order to weed out the poor students, the test maker hopes that if your child doesn't know how to solve a problem, he or she will make a mistake *before* getting to *the right choice.* So for this particular type of example the test maker usually puts the right choice at the end of the string of choices: C or D (or D or E if there is an E choice). Thus, by the time your child gets to the right choice, he or she will usually have eliminated two or three of the incorrect ones. So here's a useful strategy: For a four-choice question, *always start with Choice D, and then go to C, B, and A.*

Practice using this strategy in the following examples.

EXAMPLE 1

Which of the following sums will always be a whole number?

(A) a fraction added to a fraction
(B) a fraction added to a whole number
(C) a decimal fraction multiplied by a whole number
(D) a whole number added to a whole number

Look at Choice D first since you have to test all of the choices. A whole number added to a whole number is a whole number. To be sure, try some numbers: $1 + 2 = 3$; $2 + 3 = 5$. Choice D is correct. There is no need to look at the other choices.

EXAMPLE 2

All numbers are equal to $\frac{3}{4}$ except

(A) $\frac{9}{12}$ (B) $\frac{15}{20}$ (C) $\frac{12}{16}$ (D) $\frac{6}{9}$

Here you have to examine all of the choices, so start with Choice D. Compare $\frac{3}{4}$ with $\frac{6}{9}$. $\frac{3}{4} = \frac{6}{8}$, so it is not equal to $\frac{6}{9}$. Choice D is correct. There is no need to look at any of the other choices.

EXAMPLE 3

Which of the following can be the dimensions of a rectangular box whose volume is 50 cubic centimeters?

(A) 5 cm × 5 cm × 3 cm
(A) 4 cm × 10 cm × 2 cm
(C) 24 cm × 2 cm × 1 cm
(D) 25 cm × 2 cm × 1 cm

Look at choice D first: $25 \times 2 \times 1 = 50$. Choice D is correct. There is no need to look at the other choices.

EXAMPLE 4

$$
\begin{array}{r}
5x6 \\
+\ \ 338 \\
\hline
9y4
\end{array}
$$

If in the addition problem above, x and y represent digits from 0 to 9, what can x be?

(A) 3 (B) 4 (C) 5 (D) 6

This is an excellent illustration of the last-choice method because using it not only allows you to save a lot of time but eliminates a great deal of mental exhaustion. Try Choice D first:
Let $x = 6$: For the addition you get:

$$
\begin{array}{r}
1\ 1 \\
5\ 6\ 6 \\
+\ \ 3\ 3\ 8 \\
\hline
9\ 0\ 4
\end{array}
$$

Using $x = 6$ satisfies the addition. Choice D is correct.

Have your child work on these problems. Go over your child's answers and make sure he or she has used the strategies presented in the explanatory answers to these problems.

PROBLEMS

1 Which is always an odd number?

   (A) an odd number plus an odd number
   (B) an even number plus an even number
   (C) an odd number divided by an odd number
   (D) an odd number times an odd number

2 Which fraction is greater than $\frac{3}{7}$?

   (A) $\frac{5}{12}$ (B) $\frac{6}{14}$ (C) $\frac{8}{19}$ (D) $\frac{7}{16}$

3 If a square has a whole number for one of its sides, which of the following could be its area?

   (A) 80 (B) 66 (C) 49 (D) 32

4

$$
\begin{array}{r}
3\,5 \\
\times \quad y \\
\hline
1\ x\ 0
\end{array}
$$

In the multiplication above, x and y are integers from 0 to 9 (inclusive). What can y be?

(A) 8 (B) 6 (C) 5 (D) 4

SOLUTIONS

1 (D) Since you have to test all of the choices, start with the last one, Choice D: An odd number times an odd number. Try different examples if you're not sure of this one:

$3 \times 1 = 3$ (odd $\times$ odd = odd)
$5 \times 5 = 25$ (odd $\times$ odd = odd, again)

You can be pretty sure an odd number times an odd number is odd. There is no need to look at the other choices.

2 (D) Since you have to test all of the choices, start with Choice D. Refer to the shortcut for comparing fractions described in the "Math Shortcuts" section at the end of this book (see pages 173–182).

Comparing Choice D:

$$
\left(\frac{7}{16} \quad \diagdown\!\!\!\!\diagup \quad \frac{3}{7} \right)
$$

$$
49 \qquad 48
$$

$$
49 \ > \ 48
$$

so

$$
\frac{7}{16} \ > \ \frac{3}{7}
$$

Choice D is correct.

3 (C) You know that the area of a square is: side $\times$ side. So you are looking for a choice in which a whole number times the same whole number equals the number in the choice. Since you have to test out all of the choices, start with Choice D. What whole number times itself gives you 32? No number. Choice D is incorrect.

Now look at Choice C: What whole number times itself gives you 49. It's 7. So the square could have 7 as its side. Choice C is correct. There is no need to look at the other choices.

4 (D) Look at Choice D first. Let $y = \underline{4}$. Then

$$
\begin{array}{r}
3\,5 \\
\times \quad 4 \\
\hline
1\,4\,0
\end{array}
$$

This satisfies the multiplication where $x = 4$ and $y = 4$. So Choice D is correct.

MATH STRATEGY 6:
You Don't Always Need a Complete Solution

At times when working on the solution to a math problem, your child will get some result but not the complete answer. At that point it may still be possible to eliminate incorrect choices by comparing his or her result with the answer choices.

Here are some examples:

EXAMPLE 1

$$
\begin{array}{r}
364 \\
\times \quad 476 \\
\hline
ABCD \\
DEFG \\
HIJK \\
\hline
173264
\end{array}
$$

What is the number *HIJK?*

(A) 2,184 (B) 2,548 (C) 1,456 (D) 17,108

You should realize that *ABCD* is derived by multiplying 364×6, *DEFG* by multiplying 364×7, and *HIJK* by multiplying 364×4. So when you multiply 364×4, you end up with a number *ending in a 6*, since $4 \times 4 = 16$. The only choice that ends in a 6 is Choice C. So Choice C must be correct. Therefore you don't have to multiply out the whole product of 364×4.

EXAMPLE 2

What is the product of $1 \times 2 \times 3 \times 4 \times 5 \times 6 \times 7$?

(A) 5,039 (B) 5,040 (C) 5,041 (D) 5,042

Instead of multiplying out, just realize that the $\underline{2}$ in the problem times the $\underline{5}$ in the problem gives you $\underline{10}$. And 10 times the rest of the numbers *must end in 0*, because 10 times any integer ends in 0. Thus your correct choice must end in 0. The only one that does is Choice B. So Choice B is correct. Look at all the time you saved!

Have your child try these questions. Go over the solutions with your child to see whether he or she has used the strategies described in the book.

PROBLEMS

1 A bike is priced normally $234.95 but is reduced by 20 percent. By how much is the bike reduced by?
  (A) $46.99
  (B) $49.95
  (C) $55.88
  (D) $44.67

2 $4\overline{)4,356} =$
  (A) 1,088
  (B) 1,089
  (C) 1,090
  (D) 1,091

SOLUTIONS

1 (A) Multiply 234.95 by 20% :

$$234.95 \times \frac{20}{100}$$

$$\begin{array}{r} 234.95 \\ \times\ \ \ \ 20 \\ \hline 900 \end{array}$$

Stop here. When you move the decimal point over two places, you end up with a $\underline{9}$ as the last digit. So let's look for a $\underline{9}$ in the answer. Only Choice A has a 9 in the answer.

There is no need to multiply the whole product out.

2 (B) You should realize that these choices differ only in the last digit. Here you're looking for a number that when multiplied by 4 will give you 4,356. That number cannot end in 8 (Choice A) because $8 \times 4 = 3\underline{2}$ and the last digit of 4,356 is not 2. The number cannot end in 0 (Choice C) because $0 \times 4 = 0$, and the last digit of 4,356 ends in 6, not 0. The number cannot end in 1 (Choice D) because $1 \times 4 = 4$, which is not the last digit of 4,356. Thus only Choice B remains.

MATH STRATEGY 7:
Know How to Work with Problems Dealing with Averages

Whenever your child sees a problem that says "average," he or she should know what the word means. It is

$$\frac{\text{the sum of the values of all the items}}{\text{the total number of items}}$$

For example, the average score on a set of tests equals

$$\frac{\text{sum of all the scores}}{\text{number of tests scored}}$$

The average score of a number of students is

$$\frac{\text{sum of scores of all the students}}{\text{number of students}}$$

The average rate of a car traveling a certain distance equals

$$\frac{\text{the total distance the car traveled}}{\text{the total time the car traveled}}$$

The average of a set of numbers is

$$\frac{\text{the sum of all the numbers}}{\text{the number of numbers}}$$

As soon as you see the word "average," translate the meaning as described above. Here are some examples:

EXAMPLE 1

The average of 7, 4, and −3 is

(A) 8   (B) $4\frac{2}{3}$ (C) $2\frac{2}{3}$ (D) −1

Remember;

$$\text{average} = \frac{\text{sum of numbers}}{\text{number of numbers}}$$

So

$$\text{average} = \frac{7 + 4 - 3}{3}$$

$$= \frac{8}{3}$$

$$= 2\frac{2}{3}$$

Choice C is correct.

EXAMPLE 2

The average of 6 numbers is 10. The sum of 5 of these numbers is 40. The remaining number is

(A) 20 (B) 30 (C) 40 (D) 50

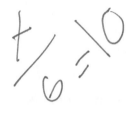

Remember:

$$\text{average} = \frac{\text{sum of values of the numbers}}{\text{number of numbers}}$$

But what do you do since you don't know the numbers? Call the numbers a, b, c, d, e, and f. Then

$$\text{average} = 10 \text{ (given)} = \frac{a+b+c+d+e+f}{6} \quad \begin{array}{l} \leftarrow \text{sum of values} \\ \leftarrow \text{number of numbers} \end{array}$$

But you know that 5 of the numbers add up to 40. So let $a + b + c + d + e = 40$. Putting the value of $a + b + c + d + e$ in the equation above you get:

$$\text{average} = 10 = \frac{a+b+c+d+e+f}{6} = \frac{40 + f}{6}$$

$$10 = \frac{40 + f}{6}$$

Multiply both sides of the equation by 6:

$$10 \times 6 = \frac{40 + f}{6} \times 6$$

$$60 = 40 + f$$

Now subtract 40 from both sides:

$$60 - 40 = 40 + f - 40$$

$$20 = f$$

The remaining number is 20. (Choice A).

EXAMPLE 3

A car travels along a straight line from A to B to C. It travels from A to B in 2 hours and from B to C in 3 hours. What is the average speed of the car in kilometers per hour if the distance from A to B is 40 km and the distance from B to C is 70 km?

(A) 55 (B) 44 (C) 33 (D) 22

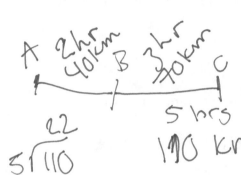

$$\text{average speed} = \frac{\text{total distance traveled}}{\text{total time for complete trip}}$$

$$\text{average speed} = \frac{40 \text{ km} + 70 \text{ km}}{2 \text{ hrs} + 3 \text{ hrs}} \quad \begin{matrix} \leftarrow \text{Total distance} \\ \leftarrow \text{Total time} \end{matrix}$$

$$= \frac{110 \text{ km}}{5 \text{ hrs}}$$

$$= 22 \text{ km/hr (Choice D)}$$

PROBLEMS

Have your child try these questions. Then check to see whether his or her answers match the ones that are given at the end of these questions. Make sure that your child uses the right strategies as explained in the explanatory answers.

1 A four-sided figure has sides of 4 cm, 4 cm, 7 cm, and 8 cm. What is the average length per side of the figure?
   (A) 23 cm
   (B) 8½ cm
   (C) 5¾ cm
   (D) 7¾ cm

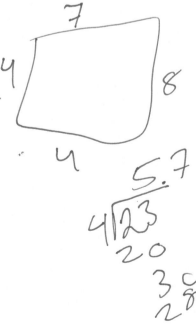

2 The average of −5, +7, +5, and −7 is
   (A) −2
   (B) +2
   (C) 0
   (D) −1

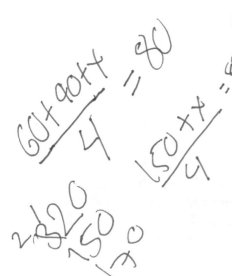

3 The average score of 4 students on a test was 80. The lowest score was 60 and the highest score was 90. What was the sum of the remaining two scores on the test?

(A) 140
(B) 150
(C) 160
(D) 170

4 A train travels from New York to Chicago in 24 hours and from Chicago to St. Louis in 16 hours. If the total distance from New York to St. Louis (straight line distance) is 1,200 miles, what was the average speed of the train for the complete trip from New York to St. Louis?

(A) 30 mph
(B) 40 mph
(C) 50 mph
(D) cannot be determined

SOLUTIONS

1 (C) Remember:

$$\text{average} = \frac{\text{total value of items (sides)}}{\text{total number of items (sides)}}$$

$$\text{average} = \frac{4 \text{ cm} + 4 \text{ cm} + 7 \text{ cm} + 8 \text{ cm}}{4}$$

$$\text{average} = \frac{23 \text{ cm}}{4}$$

$$= 5\frac{3}{4} \text{ cm (Choice C)}$$

2 (C) Remember:

$$\text{average} = \frac{\text{sum of numbers}}{\text{number of numbers}}$$

$$\text{average} = \frac{-5 + 7 + 5 - 7}{4}$$

Notice that the -5 cancels with the $+5$ and the -7 cancels with the $+7$ to give a 0 for the numerator of the average.

Thus the average $= \frac{0}{4} = 0$ (Choice C).

3 (D) Remember:

$$\text{average of scores} = \frac{\text{sum of scores}}{\text{number of students}}$$

$40\overline{)1200}$

The highest score was 90, the lowest 60. Let the other two scores be represented by a and b. So

$$\text{Average} = 80 \text{ (given)} = \frac{90 + 60 + a + b}{4} \begin{array}{l} \leftarrow \text{sum of scores} \\ \leftarrow \text{number of students} \end{array}$$

Multiply both sides of the equation by 4:

$$80 \times 4 = \frac{90 + 60 + a + b}{4} \times 4$$

$$320 = 90 + 60 + a + b$$

$$320 = 150 + a + b$$

Subtract 150 from both sides:

$$320 - 150 = 150 + a + b - 150$$

$$170 = a + b$$

But $a + b$ are the sum of scores of the remaining students, so the answer is 170. (Choice D).

4   (D) This is very tricky. The average speed is

$$\frac{\text{total distance}}{\text{total time}}$$

The total time is $24 + 16 = 40$ hours.

But the total distance is *not* 1,200 miles because the distance from New York to Chicago (as the train travels) plus the distance from Chicago to St. Louis (as the train travels) is going to be greater than the straight line distance from New York to St. Louis. (See the diagram below.) Thus you cannot determine an answer (Choice D).

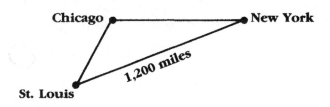

MATH STRATEGY 8:
   Label Sides, Angles, Etc., with Numbers or Letters

In questions with Diagrams, have your child label everything so that he or she can have as complete an understanding as possible of the problem. Here are some examples:

EXAMPLE 1

In the drawing below, in which all boxes are squares of equal area, the distance from *B* to *C* is 10 kilometers. What is the distance from *A* to *B*?

(A) 3 (B) 4 (C) 5 (D) 6

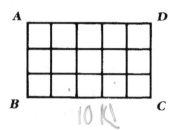

Since the distance from *B* to *C* is 10 kilometers, and there are 5 squares from *B* to *D*, each square has a side of 2. So label each side of the squares 2. Thus *AB* = 6 (Choice D).

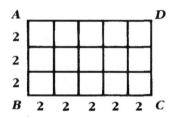

EXAMPLE 2

In the figure below, *CD* and *BC* are the same length. *ED* and *AE* are also the same length. What is the perimeter of the figure?

(A) 27 (B) 32 (C) 35 (D) 40

$CD = BC$
$ED = AE$

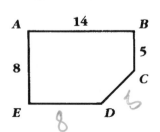

Label $CD = 5$ (since $CD = BC$) and $ED = 8$ (since $ED = AE$).

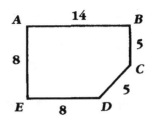

This makes the perimeter $8 + 8 + 5 + 5 + 14 = 40$ (Choice D).

EXAMPLE 3

The perimeter of an equilateral triangle is $21y$. What is the side of the triangle?

(A) $7y$ (B) $8y$ (C) $9y$ (D) $10y$

An equilateral triangle has equal sides. Label each side of the triangle s. Then perimeter $= s + s + s = 3s$. Set $3s = 21y$. Divide by 3 to get s:

$$\frac{\cancel{3}s}{\cancel{3}} = \frac{21y}{3}$$

$$s = 7y \text{ (Choice A)}$$

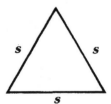

EXAMPLE 4

What is the perimeter of the parallelogram below:

(A) 23 (B) 38 (C) 46 (D) 61

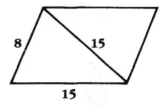

Remember: In a parallelogram the opposite sides are equal. So label each of the sides:

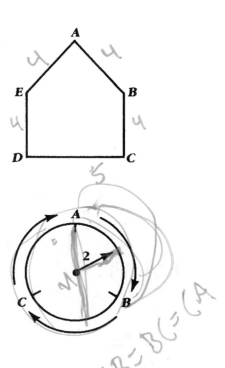

Perimeter = 15 + 8 + 15 + 8 = 46. (Choice C).

Have your child try these questions. Then check to see whether his or her answers match the ones at the end of the examples. Make sure your child uses the right approach and strategy.

PROBLEMS

1 An equilateral triangle has a perimeter of 32. What is its side?

(A) 10
(B) 16
(C) 4
(D) 10⅔

2 In this figure (right), $AB = AE = ED = BC$. $DC = 5$ and $AE = 4$. What is the perimeter of figure $ABCDE$?

(A) 9
(B) 17
(C) 18
(D) 21

3 The distance around the circumference from A to B in the circle (right), is the same as the distance around the circumference from B to C and the same as the distance around the circumference from C to A. If the radius of the circle is 2, what is the circular distance from A to B?

(A) 4π
(B) 2π
(C) $\dfrac{4\pi}{3}$
(D) $\dfrac{2\pi}{3}$

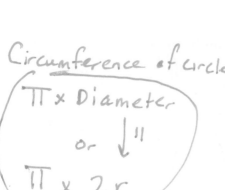

4 Each of the squares in the figure below has an equal area. If the area of the whole figure *ABCD* is 80, what is the area of each smaller square?

(A) 2
(B) 4
(C) 8
(D) 16

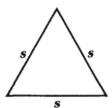

SOLUTIONS

1 (D) All of the sides of an equilateral triangle are equal. Draw and label each side of the triangle *s*:

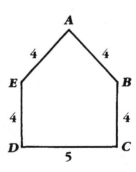

Perimeter = $s + s + s = 3s$.
But you were told that the perimeter = 32. So set $3s = 32$.
Divide by 3:

$$\frac{3s}{3} = \frac{32}{3}$$

$$s = 10\frac{2}{3}$$

2 (D) Label all sides:

Perimeter = $4 + 4 + 4 + 4 + 5 = 21$

3 (C) Label the circular distance from *A* to *B* as *a*. Since the circular distance from *B* to *C* is the same as from *C* to *A*, label the other circular distances *a* also.

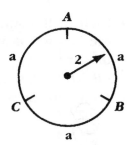

The radius of 2 tells us that the whole circumference = $2\pi(2) = 4\pi$ (since circumference = $2\pi r$). Thus circumference = 4π. But we know that $3a$ is also the circumference.

So let $4\pi = 3a$.

Divide by 3:

$$\frac{4\pi}{3} = \frac{\cancel{3}a}{\cancel{3}}$$

$$\frac{4\pi}{3} = a$$

4 (A) Label the width and length of the rectangle with number of units for length and width.

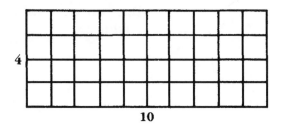

Area = length × width = 10 × 4 = 40.

So there are 40 little squares. But the area of the rectangle is 80, so each square must be $\underline{2}$ units in area if 40 squares have a total area of 80.

MATH STRATEGY 9:
Subtract Knowns from Knowns to Get Unknowns

This is a very useful strategy, especially when problems with figures are presented. Here are a few examples:

EXAMPLE 1

The area of the shaded region is

(A) 12 square meters
(B) 17 square meters
(C) 22 square meters
(D) 34 square meters

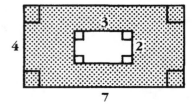

You will find that it is almost impossible to find the shaded area by some *direct* calculation. So you should say to yourself, how can I get the area from the areas that I'm given?

STRATEGY: Subtract Known Areas from Known Areas to Get Unknown Areas. The area of the *big rectangle minus the area of the smaller rectangle* will give you the area of the shaded region, because that's the area that is left over after subtracting.

The area of the big rectangle is length × width = 7 × 4 = 28
The area of the small rectangle is length × width = 3 × 2 = 6
The difference is 28 − 6 = 22. (Choice C)

Here's another example with lines, not areas:

EXAMPLE 2

What is the distance of line *AB*?

(A) 10.6 (B) 9.5 (C) 4.2 (D) cannot tell

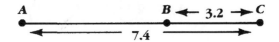

Use the same strategy, but use it for *lines*. Subtract Knowns from Knowns to Get Unknowns:

The distance of line *AB* can be found by subtracting:
$AC - BC = AB$

$AC = 7.4, BC = 3.2.$
So $AB = 7.4 - 3.2 = 4.2$ (Choice C).

EXAMPLE 3

What is the area of the shaded region if the area of the small circle is 12 and the area of the large circle is 20?

(A) 32
(B) 8
(C) 10
(D) cannot tell

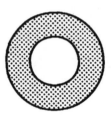

The area of the *shaded region* is found by subtracting the *area* of the *large circle from* the *area* of the *small circle.* Thus the *area* of the *shaded region* is just $20 - 12 = 8.$ (Choice B).

Have your child try these questions. Check to see whether his or her answers match those in the book, making sure that your child used the same method of solution presented there.

PROBLEMS

1 If the area of the large triangle *ABD* is 20 and the area of small triangle is 4, what is the area of shaded region?

(A) 24 (B) 16 (C) 8 (D) cannot tell

2 What is the distance *x* in the diagram below?

(A) 1 (B) 2 (C) 3 (D) 4

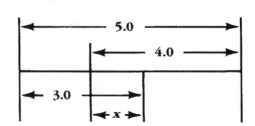

3 If the side of the square is 4 and the radius of the inscribed circle is 2, what is the area of all the shaded regions?

(A) 2 (B) $8 - 2\pi$ (C) 4 (D) $16 - 4\pi$

SOLUTIONS

1 (B) Subtract knowns from knowns to get unknowns: The area of the large triangle − the area of small triangle = the area of the shaded region. So $20 - 4 = 16$.

2 (B) Subtracting 4 from 5 $(5 - 4)$ gives you the segment to the left of the segment of length x. Now the segment of length 3 minus the segment of length 1 (the segment to the left of x) gives you what the length of x is. $(3 - 1 = 2)$.

3 (D) The area of the shaded regions is equal to the area of the square minus the area of the circle:

area of shaded regions = area of square − area of circle.

So let's find the area of the square and the area of the circle.

The area of the square = side × side = $4 \times 4 = 16$
The area of the circle = π × radius × radius = $\pi (2 \times 2) = 4\pi$

So the area of shaded regions = $16 - 4\pi$.

QUANTITATIVE COMPARISON

The quantitative comparison question has been used more and more on standardized tests. In this question, the student is asked to compare quantities in two columns. He or she is asked to find whether the quantity in the first column is greater, less than, or equal to the quantity in the second column. On exams of this level (grades 6 to 9 and up), the student is also asked to state whether in fact a determination can even be made.

Here's a very simple illustration of this:

EXAMPLE

Column A	Column B
2	1

Choose A   if the quantity in Column A is always <u>greater than</u> the quantity in Column B

Choose B   if the quantity in Column A is always <u>less than</u> the quantity in Column B

Choose C   if the quantity in Column A is always <u>equal to</u> the quantity in Column B

Choose D   if a definite comparison between Column A and Column B cannot be made (in other words if Choices A, B, and C are false).

SOLUTION

Since 2 is greater than 1, you would say Column A is greater than Column B and so Choice A is correct.

There are many questions of the quantitative comparison type much more difficult than the example above that will take a student a long time to answer and subject the student to mistakes if he or she doesn't know certain strategies.

Here are some rules that you and your child will discover for yourselves as you become more familiar with the strategies, but it's a good idea to see them now and be aware of them:

1 Never choose D if just actual numbers (no algebraic letters) are present in the columns.

2 You can always substitute numbers for the letters to see how the columns compare.

3 You can always *add* or *subtract* the *same quantity* to both columns and still get the *same comparison* between the columns.

4 You can always *multiply* or *divide both* columns by the *same positive number* and still get the *same comparison* between the columns.

QUANTITATIVE COMPARISON STRATEGY 1:
Cancel Quantities Common to Both Columns

EXAMPLE 1

Column A	Column B
124 + 376	376 + 125

Remember:

Choose A   if Column A is greater than Column B.
Choose B   if Column A is less than Column B.
Choose C   if Column A equals Column B.
Choose D   if a definite comparison cannot be made.

How do you think this problem should be approached? Should we add the 124 + 376 under Column A and then compare the sum with that of 376 + 125 under Column B? That's probably the way your child was taught to do such problems, but it's not the easiest or most direct way. Since in quantitative comparison questions you are not asked to find actual results or answers, but only to *compare* the columns, it isn't necessary to calculate what's under each column. After all, if the test maker had wanted your child just to do a straight calculation, he or she would have used the question in the regular multiple-choice math section, not in the quantitative comparison section.

Here's the strategy: *Get rid of quantities common to both columns.*

In the example above, get rid of the 376 that appears in both columns:

Column A	Column B
124 + ~~376~~	~~376~~ + 125
↓	↓

This leaves   124   125

Since 124 is less than 125, Column A is less than Column B. Choice B is therefore correct.

This strategy also works for numbers that are multiplied. For example:

EXAMPLE 2

Column A	Column B
23 × 34 × 31	34 × 31 × 22

Whatever you do, don't multiply the numbers in each column! Cancel the common 34 and 31 from both columns:

Column A	Column B
23 × 3̶4̶ × 3̶1̶	3̶4̶ × 3̶1̶ × 22
↓	↓
23	22

Column A is greater than Column B, so Choice A is correct. There's just one note of caution: Remember, in *multiplication* or *division* problems, *never cancel* if you may be canceling a *negative number* or *0*:

EXAMPLE 3

Column A	Column B
$3a$	$2a$

If you canceled the a, you would find that 3 is greater than 2 and choose A as the answer. But that's not correct. Because if $a = 0$, the *columns are equal* and if a is negative, Column A is *less than* Column B! So when using this strategy for multiplication or division problems (don't worry about addition or subtraction problems) do not cancel a negative number or cancel 0 from both columns.

The way you would do Example 3 is to try different values for a : Let $a = 0$: Then the columns are equal. Column A = Column B = 0. Let $a = 1$: Column A = 3 and Column B = 2; therefore Column A > Column B.

Since you get two different comparisons, a definite comparison of the columns cannot be made and Choice D is correct according to the directions.

More on these Choice D questions will be given later, in connection with another strategy, so if this is not completely clear now, it will become clearer later when we do more of these problems.

Have your child try the following examples. Check to see whether his or her solutions match those given in the book, making sure that your child has used the strategies described here.

Remember:

Choose A   if Column A is greater than Column B.
Choose B   if Column A is less than Column B.
Choose C   if Column A equals Column B.
Choose D   if a definite comparison cannot be made.

PROBLEMS

	Column A	Column B
1	$14 + 17 + 18 + 20$	$15 + 17 + 18 + 19$
2	$\dfrac{372}{5}$	$\dfrac{372}{5.1}$
3	$\begin{array}{r} 34 \\ \times\ 40 \end{array}$	$\begin{array}{r} 40 \\ \times\ 33 \end{array}$
4	$\dfrac{7 \times 9 \times 11 \times 13}{12}$	$\dfrac{11 \times 9 \times 7 \times 13}{15}$
5	$\begin{array}{r} 29 \\ \times\ 4 \end{array}$	$\begin{array}{r} 29 \\ 29 \\ +\ 29 \end{array}$
6	562×4	562×3.9
7	$2 + a$	$3 + a$
8	$5b$	$6b$

SOLUTIONS

1   (C) Cancel common quantities from both sides:

Column A	Column B
$14 + 17 + 18 + 20$	$15 + 17 + 18 + 19$
$14 + 20$	$15 + 19$
34	34

Column A = Column B

2 (A) Cancel common quantities:

Column A	Column B
$\dfrac{\cancel{372}}{5}$	$\dfrac{\cancel{372}}{5.1}$
$\dfrac{1}{5}$	$\dfrac{1}{5.1}$

Column A is greater.

3 (A) Write columns like this:

Column A	Column B
34×40	40×33

Now cancel common quantities from both columns:

Column A	Column B
$34 \times \cancel{40}$	$\cancel{40} \times 33$
34	33

Column A is greater than Column B.

4 (A) Cancel common quantities:

Column A	Column B
$\dfrac{\cancel{7 \times 9 \times 11 \times 13}}{12}$	$\dfrac{\cancel{11 \times 9 \times 7 \times 13}}{15}$
$\dfrac{1}{12}$	$\dfrac{1}{15}$

Column A is greater than column B

5 (A) Rewrite as:

Column A	Column B
29×4	29×3

Cancel common quantities:

Column A	Column B
$\dfrac{\cancel{29} \times 4}{4}$	$\dfrac{\cancel{29} \times 3}{3}$

Column A is greater than Column B.

6 (A) Cancel common quantities:

Column A	Column B
$\dfrac{\cancel{562} \times 4}{4}$	$\dfrac{\cancel{562} \times 3.9}{3.9}$

Column A is greater than Column B.

7 (B) Cancel a from both columns:

Column A	Column B
$\dfrac{2 + \cancel{a}}{2}$	$\dfrac{3 + \cancel{a}}{3}$

Column A is less than Column B.

8 (D) This is tricky: In multiplication you can't just cancel the b because b may be 0 or be negative.

If b is *not* 0, then $5b$ is less than $6b$.
If b is 0, then $5b = 6b$.

Thus a definite comparison cannot be made and Choice D is correct.

QUANTITATIVE COMPARISON STRATEGY 2:
To Simplify, You Can Multiply, Divide, Add, or Subtract the Same Number in Both Columns

Remember:

Choose A if Column A is greater than Column B.
Choose B if Column A is less than Column B.
Choose C if Column A equals Column B.
Choose D if a definite comparison cannot be made.

EXAMPLE 1

Column A	Column B
$1290 - 297$	1002

Instead of subtracting $1290 - 297$, add 297 to both columns:

Column A	Column B
$1290 - 297 + 297$	$1002 + 297$
1290	1299

Column A is less than Column B, so Choice B is correct. We added 297 to both columns to *get rid of the minus sign* in Column A, since it's easier to add than subtract in this case.

EXAMPLE 2

Here's a problem where you'd *subtract* instead of *add*.

Column A	Column B
$424 + 478$	$479 + 423$

Don't add yet! You can see that the 478 in Column A is just 1 unit less than the 479 in Column B. You can also see that the 424 in Column A is just 1 unit more than the 423 in Column B. Let's subtract 423 from both columns.

Column A	Column B

Subtract 423 from both columns

$$424 + 478$$
$$\downarrow$$
$$424 + 478 - \underline{423}$$
$$\downarrow$$
$$424 + 478 - 423$$
$$= 1$$
$$\downarrow$$
$$1 + 478$$
$$\downarrow$$
$$479$$

$$479 + 423$$
$$\downarrow$$
$$479 + 423 - \underline{423}$$
$$\downarrow$$
$$479 + 423 - 423$$
$$\downarrow$$
$$479$$
$$\downarrow$$
$$479$$

Column A equals Column B, so Choice C is correct.

Here are a few examples that require *multiplying* each column by the same number. (This type of problem is explained in the "Math Shortcuts" section on page 175.)

EXAMPLE 3

36

Column A	Column B
$\dfrac{4}{7}$	$\dfrac{5}{9}$

35

Use the following strategy: Try to get rid of denominators—they make things difficult. Do this by multiplying Column A and Column B by 7. This cancels the 7 in the Column A denominator:

Column A	Column B
$\dfrac{4}{7} \times 7 \; (= 4)$	$\dfrac{5}{9} \times 7$

Now multiply both columns by 9 to get rid of the denominator in Column B:

Column A	Column B
4×9	$\dfrac{5}{\cancel{9}} \times 7 \times \cancel{9}$
36	35

Column A is Greater than Column B, so Choice A is correct.

EXAMPLE 4

Column A	Column B
1	$\dfrac{\frac{3}{4}}{\frac{4}{3}}$

Don't divide 3/4 by 4/3! *Multiply* both columns by $\dfrac{4}{3}$ to get rid of the complicated numerator in Column B.

Column A	Column B
$1 \times \dfrac{4}{3}$	$\dfrac{\frac{3}{4}}{\frac{4}{3}} \times \dfrac{4}{3}$
$\dfrac{4}{3}$	$\dfrac{3}{4}$

Column A is greater than Column B and therefore Choice A is correct.

$5x \qquad\qquad\qquad\qquad 6x$

EXAMPLE 5

Column A	Column B
	x is positive
$\dfrac{2}{3}$ $\dfrac{x}{x + 1}$	$\dfrac{3}{2}$ $\dfrac{x + 1}{x}$

Multiply both columns by x and then by $x + 1$ to get rid of fractions:

Column A	Column B
Multiply by x:	
$\dfrac{x}{x + 1} \times x$	$\dfrac{x + 1}{x} \times x$
$\dfrac{(x)(x)}{x + 1}$	$x + 1$
Multiply by $x + 1$:	
$\dfrac{(x)(x)}{x + 1} \times (x + 1)$	$x + 1 (x + 1)$
$(x)(x)$	$(x + 1)(x + 1)$

Since x is positive (given), Column A is less than Column B and Choice B is correct.

In the following example, both columns should be *divided* by the same number.

EXAMPLE 6

Column A	Column B
32×35	33×34

Divide both columns by 34, and then by 32:

Column A	Column B

Divide by 34:

$$\frac{32 \times 35}{34} \qquad\qquad \frac{33 \times 34}{34}$$

$$\frac{32 \times 35}{34} \qquad\qquad 33$$

Divide by 32:

$$\frac{32 \times 35}{(34)(32)} \qquad\qquad \frac{33}{32}$$

$$\frac{35}{34} \qquad\qquad \frac{33}{32}$$

$$1\frac{1}{34} \qquad\qquad 1\frac{1}{32}$$

Column A is less than Column B, so Choice B is correct.

Have your child try the following questions. Make sure that he or she uses the method described in the book.

Remember:

Choose A if Column A is greater than Column B.
Choose B if Column A is less than Column B.
Choose C if Column A equals Column B.
Choose D if a definite comparison cannot be made.

PROBLEMS

	Column A	Column B
1	$\dfrac{4}{5} \div 4$	$\dfrac{1}{5}$
2	$\dfrac{10}{7} \div \dfrac{3}{7}$	$\dfrac{10}{3}$

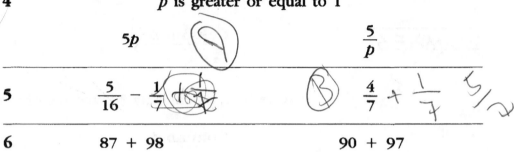

	Column A		Column B
3	4×3	12	$\dfrac{300}{25}$ 
4	p is greater or equal to 1		
	$5p$	0	$\dfrac{5}{p}$
5	$\dfrac{5}{16} - \dfrac{1}{7}$		$\dfrac{4}{7} + \dfrac{1}{7}$
6	$87 + 98$		$90 + 97$

SOLUTIONS

1 (C) Multiply by 5:

Column A	Column B
$\dfrac{4}{5} \div 4 \times 5$	$\dfrac{1}{5} \times 5$
$4 \div 4$	1

Column A equals Column B.

2 (C) Multiply by $\dfrac{3}{7}$:

Column A	Column B
$\dfrac{10}{7} \div \dfrac{3}{7} \times \dfrac{3}{7}$	$\dfrac{10}{3} \times \dfrac{3}{7}$
$\dfrac{10}{7}$	$\dfrac{10}{7}$

Column A equals Column B.

3 (C) Multiply by 25:

Column A	Column B
$4 \times 3 \times 25$	$\dfrac{300}{25} \times 25$
$4 \times 25 \times 3$	300
100×3	300

Column A equals Column B.

4 (D) Multiply by p and divide by 5:

Column A	**Column B**
$\dfrac{5p \times p}{5}$	$\dfrac{5}{p} \times \dfrac{p}{5}$
$p \times p$	1

If $p = 1$ (given), then Column A = Column B.
If $p > 1$ (given), then $p \times p > 1$, so Column A > Column B. Thus a definite relation cannot be determined.

5 (B) Don't subtract! Get rid of the minus sign by adding $\dfrac{1}{7}$ to both columns.

Column A	**Column B**
$\dfrac{5}{16} - \dfrac{1}{7}$	$\dfrac{4}{7}$

Column A	**Column B**

Add $\dfrac{1}{7}$:

Column A	**Column B**
$\dfrac{5}{16} - \dfrac{1}{7} + \dfrac{1}{7}$	$\dfrac{4}{7} + \dfrac{1}{7}$
$\dfrac{5}{16}$	$\dfrac{5}{7}$

Column A is less than Column B.

6 (B) You don't have to add the numbers in the columns! Subtract 90 from both columns and then subtract 87 from both columns:

Column A	**Column B**

Subtract 90:

Column A	**Column B**
$87 + 98 - 90$	$90 + 97 - 90$
$87 + 8$	97

Subtract 87:

8	97 − 87
8	10

Column A is less than Column B.

QUANTITATIVE COMPARISON STRATEGY 3: Use Common Sense to Answer Questions

Often common sense can be used to answer quantitative comparison questions. Your child should use common sense whenever possible instead of racking his or her brains to solve certain problems. The less "brain-racking" there is on the test, the less exhausted your child will become and the more confident he or she will be when attacking the remaining questions.

Remember:

Choose A if Column A is greater than Column B
Choose B if Column A is less than Column B
Choose C if Column A equals Column B
Choose D if a definite comparison cannot be made.

EXAMPLE 1

Column A	Column B
Length of time needed to travel 60 kilometers at 30 kilometers per hour	Length of time needed to travel 40 kilometers at 30 kilometers per hour

It is obvious that it would take longer to travel 60 kilometers than it would to travel 40 kilometers, if your rate of travel (30 kph) is the same. There is no need to memorize any formulas about rate and time. Choice A is correct.

EXAMPLE 2

Column A	Column B
Circumference of circle	Perimeter of triangle

Since the shortest distance between any two points is a straight line, each of the sides of the triangle has a shorter distance than the arc of the circle it cuts. So the sum of all the arcs (the whole circle) must be larger than the sum of the sides of the triangle (the perimeter of the triangle). Choice A is correct.

EXAMPLE 3

Column A	Column B
Number of days in 7 months and 6 weeks	Number of days in 6 months and 7 weeks

It should be clear that since a month is almost four times longer than a week, 7 months and 6 weeks is longer than 6 months and 7 weeks. There is no need to calculate the exact amount of days. Choice A is correct.

EXAMPLE 4

Column A	Column B
Area of circle of radius 3	Area of circle of radius 6

Common sense: The area of a circle with the smaller radius is smaller. Column A is less than Column B. Choice B is correct.

EXAMPLE 5

Column A	Column B
Age of Harry if Harry's sister is 12 years old	Age of Mary if Mary's brother is 13 years old

Common sense: If Harry's sister is 12, that doesn't tell Harry's age. Similarly, if Mary's brother is 13, that doesn't tell Mary's age. A definite comparison between Harry's age and Mary's age cannot be made. Choice D is correct.

EXAMPLE 6

Column A	Column B
A number Q if Q is greater than 6	A number P if P is greater than 8

If Q is greater than 6, it can be any number greater than 6.
If P is greater than 8, it can be any number greater than 8.
Any number greater than 6 can be greater than, less than, or equal to a number greater than 8. Thus a definite comparison cannot be made. Choice D is correct.

EXAMPLE 7

Column A	Column B
The average of 5, 5, 5, 5, and 2	The average of 2, 2, 2, 2, and 5

Use common sense: The average of 5, 5, 5, 5, and 2 is

$$\frac{5 + 5 + 5 + 5 + 2}{5}$$

The average of 2, 2, 2, 2, 5 is

$$\frac{2 + 2 + 2 + 2 + 5}{5}$$

You can see that four 5's and a 2 is greater than four 2's and a 5 without going through the addition or division. Column A is greater than Column B, and Choice A is correct.

Have your child try the following examples. Check to see whether his or her solutions match those given in the book. Make sure your child used the strategies presented here.

Remember:

Choose A if Column A is greater than Column B
Choose B if Column A is less than Column B
Choose C if Column A equals Column B
Choose D if a definite comparison cannot be made.

PROBLEMS

	Column A		Column B
1	What is left of Mary's allowance after she spent $\frac{1}{3}$ of her allowance		What is left from Paul's allowance after he spent $\frac{1}{4}$ of his allowance
2	A whole number that is less than 6		A whole number that is greater than 5
3	3.2		2.3
4	Sam's wages if he makes 3 times as much as Phil		Phil's wages if he makes 3 times as much as Don

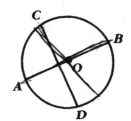

Center of Circle = O

5	length of segment *CD*		length of segment *AB*
6	The average of 17 and 31		The average of 17, 20, and 31
7	The number of odd numbers greater than 4 but less than 100		The number of even numbers greater than 4 but less than 100

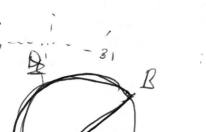

SOLUTIONS

1 (D) You don't know what Mary's allowance is, so $\frac{1}{3}$ of her allowance is not determined. What's left is also not determined. The same situation applies to what's left for Paul's allowance. Thus a comparison of the columns cannot be made.

2 (B) Think, a whole number that is less than 6 is 5, 4, 3 etc.
A whole number greater than 5 is 6, 7, 8, etc.
Any number in Column A is less than any number in Column B.

3 (A) 3.2 is greater than 2.3, so Column A is greater than Column B.

4 (A) Let Phil's wages = P. So in column A, Sam's wages are 3P.
In Column B, Phil's wages are P. 3P>P, so Column A>Column B.

5 (B) You should realize that if *AB* is a diameter of the circle (it passes through the center *O*), any chord that is not a diameter, like *CD* is going to be shorter in length. So Column A is less than Column B.

6 (A) You should realize that the average of 17 and 31 is somewhere between 17 and 31. In Column B, however, the average of 17, 20, and 31 is going to be closer to the 17 than to the 31 because the 20 is going to drag the average down toward the 17. Thus the average of 17 and 31 is greater (Column A is greater than Column B.)

7 (A) This problem is tricky. Look at all of the odd numbers greater than 4 but less than 100:

5, 7, 9 . . . all the way up to 99.

Then look at all of the even numbers:

6, 8, 10 . . . all the way up to 98.

Now write the even numbers below the odd numbers:

$$5 \quad 7 \quad 9 \quad \ldots \quad 97 \quad 99$$
$$\downarrow \quad \downarrow \quad \downarrow \quad \quad \downarrow$$
$$6 \quad 8 \quad 10 \quad \ldots \quad 98$$

You can see that there is one less even number than odd number.
So Column A is greater than Column B.

QUANTITATIVE COMPARISON STRATEGY 4: Try Numbers for Variables/Try to Get Different Comparisons

If you are given a comparison with variables like x or y in the columns, you may want to substitute numbers for them. Often a definite comparison is not possible. If you get different comparisons (like Column A > Column B and Column A = Column B), then a definite relationship cannot be made and Choice D is correct. The way to show that Choice D is correct is to choose numbers that give you comparisons like Column A > Column B. Then try to get another set of numbers for the variables, making something like Column A < Column B, or Column A = Column B. Then you will have proven that Choice D is correct.

Remember:

Choose A if Column A is greater than Column B
Choose B if Column A is less than Column B
Choose C if Column A equals Column B
Choose D if a definite comparison cannot be made.

EXAMPLE 1

Column A	Column B
A whole number less than 5	A whole number less than 2

Choose numbers consistent with what is given.
Let Column A = 4 and Column B = 1. Then Column A > Column B.
Now let Column A = 1 and Column B = 1. Then Column A = Column B.
You got two *different* comparisons. Thus Choice D is correct.

EXAMPLE 2

Column A	Column B
The value of x if $x + y = 2$	The value of y if $x + y = 2$

Choose numbers for x and y.
Let $x = 1$. Then since $x + y = 2$, $y = 1$. Column A = Column B.
Now let $x = 2$. Then since $x + y = 2$, $y = 0$, so Column A > Column B.
Two different comparisons were made, so Choice D is correct.

EXAMPLE 3

Column A	Column B

a, b, and c are consecutive whole numbers where a is smallest and c is greatest.

$$c + 1 \qquad\qquad\qquad a + 3$$

Let the consecutive numbers be 1, 2, and 3. c is greatest, so $c = 3$. a is smallest, so $a = 1$.

Column A $= c + 1 = 3 + 1 = 4$

Column B $= a + 3 = 1 + 3 = 4$

Column A = Column B.

Now choose another set of numbers. Let the consecutive whole numbers be 2, 3, 4. $a = 2$ and $c = 4$.

So Column A $= c + 1 = 4 + 1 = 5$ and

Column B $= a + 3 = 2 + 3 = 5$.

Column A = Column B again. You'd be on safe ground selecting Choice C.

EXAMPLE 4

Column A	Column B
length of segment BC	length of segment CD

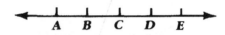

Segments AC and CE have equal lengths

Figure not drawn to scale

Choose a number for the lengths.

Let $AC = 5$ and $CE = 5$. Since the figure is not drawn to scale, BC could equal something like 2 and CD could equal something like 3, making Column A < Column B.

Or BC could equal 3 and CD could equal 2, making Column A > Column B.

Thus a definite comparison cannot be obtained and Choice D is correct.

EXAMPLE 5

Column A	Column B

y is greater than 0

 $10\, y$ $\qquad\qquad\qquad \dfrac{10}{y}$

Choose numbers for y. Let $y = 1$. Then Column A $= 10 =$ Column B.

Now let $y = 10$. Then Column A $= 100$ and Column B $= 1$, so Column A > Column B. Choice D is correct.

Have your child try the following examples. Check to see whether his or her solutions match those given in the book. Make sure your child uses the strategies presented here.

Remember:

Choose A if Column A is greater than Column B
Choose B if Column A is less than Column B
Choose C if Column A equals Column B
Choose D if a definite comparison cannot be made.

Column A	Column B
1 A whole number less than 20	A whole number greater than 19

2

x is greater than 0

x	$\dfrac{1}{x}$

3   The perimeter of the square   The perimeter of the triangle

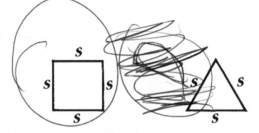

4

$$x + y = 20$$

The value of x The value of y

5   The ratio of a to $b = 2$

a 2

SOLUTIONS

1 (B) Try different numbers.

Column A	Column B
19	20

Column A < Column B
Try another set:

Column A	Column B
5	22

Column A < Column B
It would be safe to say that Column A < Column B.

2 (D) Try $x = 1$

Column A	**Column B**
1	1

Column A = Column B
Try $x = 100$

Column A	**Column B**
100	$\dfrac{1}{100}$

Column A > Column B
A definite comparison cannot be made.

3 (A) Let $s = 1$: Column A = $4s = 4 \times 1 = 4$
Column B = $3s = 3 \times 1 = 3$
Column A > Column B
Let $s = 2$: Column A = $4s = 4 \times 2 = 8$
Column B = $3s = 3 \times 2 = 6$
Column A > Column B.
It's safe to say that Column A > Column B.

4 (D) Since $x + y = 20$, let $x = 1$. Then $y = 19$.
Column A = 1, Column B = 19; Column A < Column B.
Let $x = 19$. Then $y = 1$ (this is because $x + y = 20$).
So Column A = 19, Column B = 1; Column A > Column B.
You got two different comparisons, so Choice D is correct.

5 (D) Translate: The ratio of a to b is 2: $\dfrac{a}{b} = 2$.

Let $a = 2$. Then $b = 1$, satisfying $\dfrac{a}{b} = 2$.

Column A = Column B.

Let $a = 4$. Then $b = 2$, satisfying $\dfrac{a}{b} = 2$.

Column A > Column B.
Thus a definite comparison cannot be made.

MATH REFRESHER/REVIEW
(Essential Math Skills)

Math Words, Concepts, and Rules Your Child Should Know

The following are some basic math terms and principles that your child will need to know in order to understand many of the questions on math tests.

WORDS

TRIANGLE. Any three-sided figure.

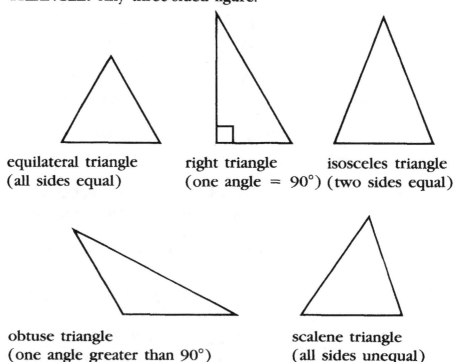

equilateral triangle   right triangle   isosceles triangle
(all sides equal)   (one angle = 90°)   (two sides equal)

obtuse triangle   scalene triangle
(one angle greater than 90°)   (all sides unequal)

RECTANGLE. Four-sided figure with opposite sides equal and parallel. Sides must meet at right angles.

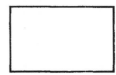

SQUARE. Four-sided figure—all, four sides equal; opposite sides parallel. Sides meet at right angles.

PARALLELOGRAM. Four-sided figure with opposite sides equal and parallel. Sides do not have to meet at right angles as in a rectangle.

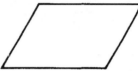

CIRCLE. A closed curve whose distance from a central point to any point on the curve is always the same. This distance is called the *radius*. The distance around the curve itself is known as the *circumference*. The *diameter* is twice the radius.

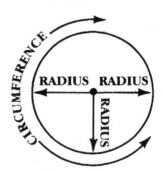

PERIMETER. Perimeter means the *length around* a figure.

EXAMPLES

Perimeter of triangle = sum of sides = 3 + 4 + 5 = 12

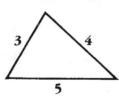

Perimeter of rectangle = sum of sides = 3 + 4 + 3 + 4 = 14

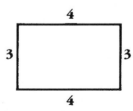

Perimeter of square = sum of sides = 4 + 4 + 4 + 4 = 16 (or 4 × 4 = 16)

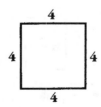

Perimeter of parallelogram = sum of sides = 3 + 4 + 3 + 4 = 14

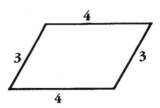

AREA OF RECTANGLE. The area of a rectangle equals its length times its width.

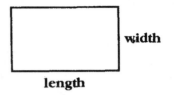

EXAMPLE

Area = length × width = 4 × 3 = 12

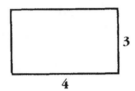

AREA OF SQUARE. The area of a square equals its length times its width.

(length = width)

EXAMPLE

Area = length × width = 3 × 3 = 9

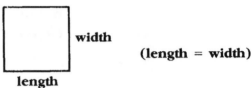

VOLUME OF RECTANGULAR BOX. The volume of a rectangular box equals its length times width times height.

Volume = length × width × height

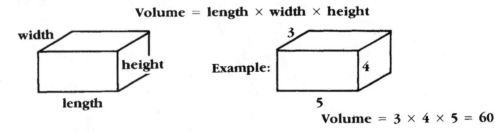

Example:

Volume = 3 × 4 × 5 = 60

AREA OF PARALLELOGRAM. The area of a parallelogram equals its base times its height.

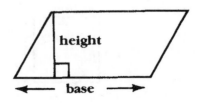

EXAMPLE

Area = 5 × 3 = 15

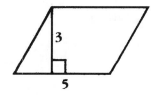

AREA OF TRIANGLE. The area of a triangle equals one half of its base times its height.

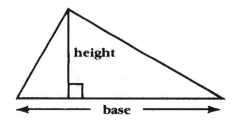

EXAMPLE

Area = $\frac{1}{2}$ × 5 × 10 = $\frac{1}{2}$ × 50 = 25

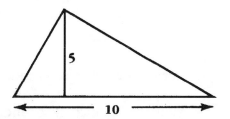

AREA OF CIRCLE. The area of a circle equals the square of its radius times pi (πr^2).

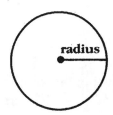

Area = $\pi (r \times r)$

π is about 3.14 or about $\frac{22}{7}$.

EXAMPLE

What is the area of a circle whose radius is 5?

Solution:

$$\begin{aligned} \text{Area} &= \pi (r \times r) \ (r = \text{radius}) \\ &= \pi (5 \times 5) \\ &= \pi (25) \\ &= 25\pi \end{aligned}$$

EXAMPLE

What is the approximate area of a circle whose radius is 7?

Solution:

$$Area = \pi \, (r \times r)$$
$$= \pi \, (7 \times 7)$$
$$\pi = \frac{22}{7} \text{ so}$$

$$Area = \frac{22}{7} \, (7 \times 7)$$

$$= \frac{22}{\not{7}} \times \not{7} \times 7 = 22 \times 7 = 154$$

PERIMETER OF CIRCLE (Circumference). The perimeter of a circle (its circumference) equals its radius times pi times 2 ($2\pi r$).

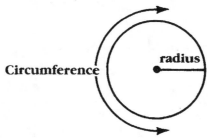

Perimeter (circumference) = $2\pi r$ (r = radius).

EXAMPLE

What is the circumference of a circle with a radius of 5?

Solution:

$$C = 2\pi r$$
$$= 2\pi \, (5)$$
$$= 10\pi$$

EXAMPLE

What is the approximate circumference of a circle with a radius of 7? (Use $\frac{22}{7}$ for π).

Solution:

$$C = 2\pi r$$
$$C = 2\pi \, (7)$$
$$C = 2 \left(\frac{22}{7}\right) 7$$

$$= 2 \left(\frac{22}{\not{7}}\right) \not{7}$$

$$= 2 \times 22$$
$$= 44$$

NUMBER LINES. A number line is a line showing increasing or decreasing numbers.

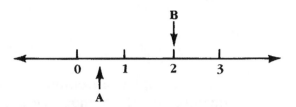

For example, on the number line above the arrow A points to 0.5, whereas the arrow B points to 2.

EXAMPLE

What does the arrow point to on the number line below?

(A) 2.1
(B) 2.2
(C) 2.3
(D) 2.4

Answer: (D) 2.4. The markings between 2 and 3 are divided equally. Since $3 - 2 = 1$, each marking represents $\frac{1}{5}$ or .2. Thus the arrow must point to 2.4.

GREATER THAN, LESS THAN, AND EQUAL TO SYMBOLS

Greater than can be written as $>$.
Less than can be written as $<$.
Equal to can be written as $=$.

EXAMPLES

$300 > 299$ (300 is *greater than* 299)
$299 < 300$ (299 is *less than* 300)
$300 = 300$ (300 is *equal to* 300)

Notice that $300 > 299$ can also be written as $299 < 300$ (299 is *less than* 300) and $299 < 300$ can also be written as $300 > 299$ (300 is *greater than* 299).

From two unequal relations, you can sometimes find a third relation. Example: Mary $>$ Sam, and Sam $>$ John.
Then Mary $>$ John.

What this really says is that if the *first is greater than the second* and the *second is greater than the third*, then the *first is greater than the third.*

FRACTIONS

A fraction has a *numerator* and a *denominator*. The numerator is on top, and the denominator is on the bottom. The numerator is *divided* by the denominator.

EXAMPLE

$$\frac{3}{7}$$

↙ numerator

← division sign

↖ denominator

When fractions have the *same numerator* but *different denominators*, the one with the *larger denominator is smaller.*

Example: $\frac{1}{8} < \frac{1}{4}$

When fractions with the *same denominator* but *different numerators*, the fraction with the *larger numerator* is *larger.*

Example: $\frac{3}{7} > \frac{2}{7}$

You can *multiply both numerator and denominator* by the *same number* and *not change the value of the fraction.*

Example: $\frac{3}{4}$

$$\frac{3}{4} \times \frac{3}{3} = \frac{9}{12}; \frac{9}{12} = \frac{3}{4}$$

EQUALS (Rules for Adding, Subtracting, Multiplying, and Dividing)

1. Equals Added to Equals Are Equal.
   Example:

$$\begin{array}{r} 3 = 3 \\ + \ 4 = 4 \\ \hline 7 = 7 \end{array}$$

2. Equals Subtracted from Equals Are Equal.
Example:

$$\begin{array}{r} 4 = 4 \\ - \; 3 = 3 \\ \hline 1 = 1 \end{array}$$

3. You Can Multiply Equals by Equals to Get Equals.
Example:

$$\begin{array}{r} 3 = 3 \\ \times \; 2 = 2 \\ \hline 6 = 6 \end{array}$$

4. You Can Divide Equals by Equals to Get Equals.
Example:

$$\begin{array}{r} 6 = 6 \\ \div \; 2 = 2 \\ \hline 3 = 3 \end{array}$$

EVEN AND ODD INTEGERS (Rules for Adding, Subtracting, Multiplying, and Dividing)

An *even integer* is a whole number *exactly divisible by 2* (2, 4, 6, 8, 10, 12, etc.). An *odd integer* is a whole number *not exactly divisible by 2* (1, 3, 5, 7, 9, 11, etc.).

1 An *even integer* plus or minus another even integer always equals an *even integer*.
For example: $4 + 6 = 10$; $6 - 4 = 2$.

2 An *even integer* plus or minus an *odd integer* always equals an *odd integer*.
For example: $4 + 1 = 5$; $4 - 3 = 1$.

3 An *odd integer* plus or minus another *odd integer* always equals an *even integer*.
For example: $3 + 5 = 8$; $9 - 5 = 4$.

4 An *even integer* multiplied by an *even integer* always equals an *even integer*.
For example: $2 \times 4 = 8$; $4 \times 4 = 16$.

5 An *even integer* multiplied by an *odd integer* always equals an *even integer*.
For example: $2 \times 3 = 6$.

6 An *odd integer* multiplied by an *odd integer* always equals an *odd integer*.
For example: $3 \times 3 = 9$; $5 \times 7 = 35$.

7 An *even integer* divided by an *even integer* is *sometimes even*, *sometimes odd*, and *sometimes not an integer*.
For example: $4 \div 2 = 2$; $12 \div 4 = 3$; $10 \div 4 = 2\frac{1}{2}$; $4 \div 8 = 1/2$.

8 An *even integer* divided by an *odd integer* is *sometimes even*, *never odd*, or *not an integer*.
For example; $2 \div 1 = 2$; $2 \div 3 = 2/3$; $12 \div 3 = 4$; $12 \div 11 = 12/11$.

9 An *odd integer* divided by an *odd integer* is *never even*, *sometimes odd*, or *not an integer*.
For example: $9 \div 3 = 3$; $11 \div 9 = 11/9$.

10 An *odd integer* divided by an *even integer* is *never an integer*.
For example: $3 \div 2 = 3/2$; $5 \div 4 = 5/4$.

AVERAGES

Average means the *total number of one group of items* divided by *the number of another group of items.*

Example 1:
There are 200 students in a school with 10 classes. What is the *average number* of students in each class?

Solution:

$$\text{Average} = \frac{\text{Total numbers of students}}{\text{Number of classes}}$$

Total number of students $= 200$
Number of classes $= 10$

$$\text{So average} = \frac{200 \text{ students}}{10 \text{ classes}} = 20 \text{ students per class}$$

Example 2:

What is the average number of melons for each crate if there are 100 melons in 10 crates?

Solution:

Total number of melons = 100
Number of crates = 10

So average $= \dfrac{100}{10} = 10$

PARTS

Example:

$\dfrac{1}{4}$ means 1 in 4 or 1 part in 4 parts.

Solution:

$\dfrac{1}{4}$ ← part of whole
   ← number of parts

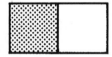

Example:

What part of the rectangle is shaded?

Solution:

1/2. Since there are *two* parts (shaded and unshaded) and *one* part is shaded, so 1/2 is shaded.

NEGATIVE NUMBERS

How to Add Negative Numbers

Examples:

1. $-2 - 5 = -7$
   (Add $2 + 5$, then put $-$ in front.)
2. $-2 + 5 = +3$
   (This is the same as $5 - 2 = 3$.)

How to Subtract Negative Numbers

Examples:

1. $-2 - (-5) = -2 + 5 = +3$
   (The $- (-5)$ becomes $+5$.)
2. $-(-2) + 3 = +2 + 3 = 5$
   (The $- (-2)$ becomes $+2$.)

How to Multiply Negative Numbers

Rules:

$$- \times - = +$$
$$- \times + = -$$
$$+ \times - = -$$
$$+ \times + = +$$

Examples:

$$-2 \times -3 = +6$$
$$-2 \times +3 = -6$$
$$+2 \times -3 = -6$$
$$+2 \times +3 = +6$$

Examples:

1. $3 \times (-5) = -15$
   (Multiply 3×5, put $-$ in front.)
2. $-3 \times -5 = +15$
   (Multiply 3×5, then multiply $- \times -: - \times - = +$.)
3. $-5 \times +3 = -15$
   (Multiply 5×3, put $-$ in front since $- \times + = -$.

How to Divide Negative Numbers

Rules:

$$\frac{+}{+} = +$$

$$\frac{+}{-} = -$$

$$\frac{-}{+} = -$$

$$\frac{-}{-} = +$$

Examples:

$$\frac{+4}{+2} = +2$$

$$\frac{+4}{-2} = -2$$

$$\frac{-4}{+2} = -2$$

$$\frac{-4}{-2} = +2$$

$$\frac{-7 + 10}{-4} = \frac{+3}{-4} = -\frac{3}{4}$$

$$\frac{-8 - 10}{-2} = \frac{-18}{-2} = +9$$

$$\frac{+8 - 10}{-2} = \frac{-2}{-2} = +1$$

$$\frac{+8 - 10}{2} = \frac{-2}{+2} = -1$$

FACTORING

Examples:

$2(3 + 4) =$

$2(3 + 4) =$

$= 2 \times 3 + 2 \times 4$

$2(4 - 3) =$

$2(4 - 3) =$

$= 2 \times 4 - 2 \times 3$

$2(3) + 2(4) = 2 \times 3 + 2 \times 4 = 6 + 8 = 14$

$2(-3) + 2(-4) = 2 \times (-3) + 2 \times (-4)$
$= -6 - 8 = -14$

$2(27 - 21) = 2(6) = 12$

$(27 - 21 = 6)$

SQUARE ROOTS

Example:
$\sqrt{25}$ means what positive number multiplied by *itself* will give you 25. It is 5.

Example:
$\sqrt{49} = 7$ since $7 \times 7 = 49$

Example:
$\sqrt{19}$ is between 4 and 5 since $4 \times 4 = 16$ and $5 \times 5 = 25$ (19 is between 16 and 25)

SQUARES

Examples:

$2^2 = 4$ since $2^2 = 2 \times 2$

$3^2 = 9$ since $3^2 = 3 \times 3$

A square of a number is that number multiplied by itself.

Example:

$$(-2)^2 = -2 \times -2 = +4$$

After you have explained to your child the words, concepts, and rules just described, have him or her try the following exercises.

PROBLEMS

1 The perimeter of the triangle below is
  (A) 480
  (B) 48
  (C) 24
  (D) 12

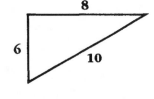

2 Which figure does *not* always have two opposite sides equal?
  (A) a parallelogram
  (B) a triangle
  (C) a rectangle
  (D) a square

3 What is the *perimeter* of the square below?
  (A) 3
  (B) 12
  (C) 9
  (D) cannot tell

4 What is the *area* of the rectangle below?
  (A) 7
  (B) 14
  (C) 12
  (D) 10

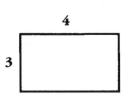

5 Which is true?
  (A) 23 > 32
  (B) 32 > 31
  (C) 33 > 35
  (D) 30 > 30

6 Which is true?
  (A) 30 < 50
  (B) 31 < 21
  (C) 21 < 21
  (D) 15 < 14

7 If $4 = 3 + \square$, then which is true?
(A) $4 - 3 = \square$
(B) $4 + 3 = \square$
(C) $4 \times 3 = \square$
(D) $4 \div 3 = \square$

8 If $3 = \square$, then which is true?
(A) $3 \times 2 = 2 \times \square$
(B) $3 \times 2 = 2 + \square$
(C) $3 \times 2 = 2 - \square$
(D) $3 \times 2 = 3 - \square$

9 Which is an even integer?
(A) 3
(B) 7
(C) 9
(D) 12

10 Which is an odd integer?
(A) 2
(B) 4
(C) 8
(D) 9

11 Which is true?
(A) $\dfrac{2}{3} > \dfrac{2}{1}$
(B) $\dfrac{3}{4} > \dfrac{3}{2}$
(C) $\dfrac{4}{7} > \dfrac{4}{8}$
(D) $\dfrac{5}{8} > \dfrac{6}{8}$

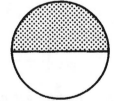

12 Which is true?
(A) $\dfrac{2}{3} = \dfrac{6}{8}$
(B) $\dfrac{3}{4} = \dfrac{9}{10}$
(C) $\dfrac{3}{5} = \dfrac{6}{12}$
(D) $\dfrac{4}{7} = \dfrac{8}{14}$

13 What is the average number of crayons per box if there are 30 boxes of crayons and a total of 900 crayons in all the boxes?
(A) 30
(B) 3
(C) 90
(D) 9

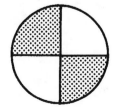

14 Which circle has 1/4 of its area shaded?

(A)
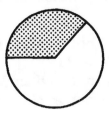

(B)

(C)

(D)

SOLUTIONS

1 (C) Perimeter equals length around.
length around = 6 + 8 + 10 = 24

2 (B) Choices:

(A) A parallelogram always has opposite sides equal.

(B) A triangle does not always have opposite sides equal.

(C) A rectangle always has opposite sides equal.

(D) A square always has opposite sides equal.

3 (B) Perimeter equals length around.
All sides of a square are equal.
So 3 + 3 + 3 + 3 = 12 or 3 × 4 = 12

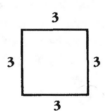

4 (C) Area of rectangle equals length times width.
length = 4, width = 3
so 4 × 3 = 12

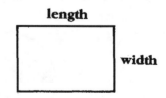

5 (B) The sign > means greater than; < means less than.
Choices:

(A) 23 is not > 32; it is < 32
(B) 32 is > 31
(C) 33 is not > than 35; it is < 35
(D) 30 is not > 30; it is = 30

6 (A) The sign < means less than; > means greater than.
Choices:

(A) 30 is < 50
(B) 31 is not < 21; 31 > 21
(C) 21 is not < 21; 21 = 21
(D) 15 is not < 14; 15 > 14

7 (A) Equals subtracted from equals are equal.

$$4 = 3 + \square$$
subtract: $\quad 3 = 3$
$$4 - 3 = \cancel{3} + \square - \cancel{3}$$

8 (A) Equals multiplied by equals are equal.

$$3 = \square$$
$$\times 2 = 2$$
$$3 \times 2 = 2 \times \square$$

9 (D) An even integer is a whole number exactly divisible by 2.
Choices:

(A) The number 3 is *not* exactly divisible by 2, so it is *odd.*
(B) The number 7 is *not* exactly divisible by 2, so it is *odd*
(C) The number 9 is *not* exactly divisible by 2, so it is *odd*
(D) The number 12 *is* exactly divisible by 2: $12 \div 2 = 6$. So it is *even.*

10 (D) An odd integer is a whole number *not* divisible by 2.
Choices:

(A) The number 2 *is* divisible by 2, so it is *even.*
(B) The number 4 *is* divisible by 2, so it is *even.*
(C) The number 8 *is* divisible by 2, so it is *even.*
(D) The number 9 *is not* divisible by 2, so it is *odd.*

11 (C) Choices:

(A) Numerators are the same, denominator 3 is larger, so $\frac{2}{3} < \frac{2}{1}$.

(B) Numerators are the same, denominator 4 is larger, so $\frac{3}{4} < \frac{3}{2}$.

(C) Numerators are the same, denominator 7 is smaller, so $\frac{4}{7} > \frac{4}{8}$.

(D) Denominators are the same, numerator 5 is smaller, so $\frac{5}{8} < \frac{6}{8}$.

12 (D) Multiply both numerator and denominator of Choice A, B by 3; of Choice C and D by 2. See "Fractions" section on page 175.

$$\frac{4}{7} \times \frac{2}{2} = \frac{8}{14}$$

Choices:

(A) $\frac{2}{3} \times \frac{3}{3} = \frac{6}{9}$ *not* $\frac{6}{8}$

(B) $\frac{3}{4} \times \frac{3}{3} = \frac{9}{12}$ *not* $\frac{9}{10}$

(C) $\frac{3}{5} \times \frac{2}{2} = \frac{6}{10}$ *not* $\frac{6}{12}$

(D) $\frac{4}{7} \times \frac{2}{2} = \frac{8}{14}$

13 (A)

$$\text{Average} = \frac{\text{Total}}{\text{Number of items}}$$

Total = 900 crayons

Number of items = 30 boxes

$$\text{Average} = \frac{900}{30} = \frac{900}{30} = 30$$

14 (B)

The fraction $\frac{1}{4}$ means 1 part in 4 parts. Of the four parts of the circle, one is shaded, so $\frac{1}{4}$ of the circle is said to be shaded.

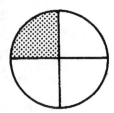

Math Shortcuts Your Child Should Know

There are many shortcuts that your child can use when working out math problems. The most important of these are discussed below.

COMPARING TWO FRACTIONS

Sometimes your child will have to find out which of two fractions is larger. Here's a typical example:

EXAMPLE

Which is greater:

$$\frac{3}{7} \text{ or } \frac{7}{16}?$$

You or your child may have been taught to find a common denominator first, and then compare the fractions. There's a much easier way that you should be aware of:

SOLUTION

$$\left(\frac{3}{7} \underset{\text{Multiply}}{\overset{\text{Multiply}}{\times}} \frac{7}{16} \right)$$

$$16 \times 3 \qquad\qquad 7 \times 7$$
$$\downarrow \qquad\qquad\qquad \downarrow$$
$$48 \qquad\qquad\qquad 49$$

Since 48 is less than 49, $\frac{3}{7}$ (above 48) is less than $\frac{7}{16}$ (above 49).

Any two fractions can be compared in this way. Try it yourself:

EXAMPLE

Which is greater:

$$\frac{4}{9} \text{ or } \frac{9}{20}?$$

SOLUTION

$$\left(\frac{4}{9} \underset{\text{Multiply}}{\overset{\text{Multiply}}{\times}} \frac{9}{20} \right)$$
$$80 \qquad\qquad\qquad 81$$

Since 80 is less than 81, $\frac{4}{9}$ is less than $\frac{9}{20}$.

ADDING FRACTIONS

EXAMPLE	What is $\frac{3}{5} + \frac{5}{7}$?

SOLUTION	Here's the quick way to add fractions:

$$\left(\frac{3}{5} \overset{\text{Multiply}}{\underset{\text{Multiply}}{\times}} \frac{5}{7} \right)$$

$$3 \times 7 \quad + \quad 5 \times 5 \; = \; \text{numerator}$$

$$\frac{3}{5} \; \underset{\text{Multiply}}{+} \; \frac{5}{7}$$

$$5 \times 7 = 35 = \text{denominator}$$

$$\text{Result} = \frac{\text{numerator}}{\text{denominator}} = \frac{(3 \times 7) + (5 \times 5)}{35} = \frac{46}{35} = 1\frac{11}{35}$$

SUBTRACTING FRACTIONS

EXAMPLE 1	Find: $\frac{5}{7} - \frac{3}{5}$

$$\left(\frac{5}{7} \overset{\text{Multiply}}{\underset{\text{Multiply}}{\times}} \frac{3}{5} \right)$$

$$25 - 21 = 4 = \text{numerator}$$

$$\frac{5}{7} - \frac{3}{5}$$

$$\underset{\text{Multiply}}{} $$

$$35 = \text{denominator}$$

$$\text{Result} = \frac{\text{numerator}}{\text{denominator}} = \frac{4}{35}$$

EXAMPLE 2	What is $2 - \frac{1}{9}$?

Write 2 as $\frac{2}{1}$.

$$\frac{2}{1} - \frac{1}{9} = \left(\frac{2}{1} \times \frac{1}{9} \right)$$

$$18 - 1 = 17 = \text{numerator}$$

$$1 \times 9 = \text{denominator}$$

So, the result is $\frac{17}{9}$, or $1\frac{8}{9}$.

MULTIPLYING FRACTIONS

When multiplying fractions, always try to reduce first.

EXAMPLE

Find: $\frac{1}{4} \times \frac{8}{33}$

Don't multiply 4×33!

$$\frac{1}{\cancel{4}} \times \frac{\cancel{8}^{2}}{33} = \frac{2}{33}$$

CALCULATING PERCENTS—IT IS SOMETIMES EASIER TO MULTIPLY RATHER THAN DIVIDE

EXAMPLE

What percent is $\frac{4}{25}$?

A percent is a number divided by 100. For example, 20% or 20 percent is $\frac{20}{100}$ So we want to find what number divided by 100 is equal to $\frac{4}{25}$.

You might be tempted to divide 25 into 4. But it is always easier to multiply than to divide. So do this:

$$\frac{4}{25} \times \frac{4}{4} = \frac{16}{100} = 16\% \text{ or } 16 \text{ percent}$$

Isn't that easier than dividing 25 into 4?

SUBTRACTING LARGE NUMBERS

EXAMPLE 1

$112 - 98 = ?$

You can do this mentally (not on paper) by saying to yourself:

$$112 - 100 = 12$$
$$100 - 98 = 2$$

Now just add 12 and 2 to get 14, and that's the answer.

The reason this works is because $112 - 100 + 100 - 98 = 112 - 98$.

EXAMPLE 2

What is $72 - 39$?

Solution:

$$72 - 42 = 30$$
$$42 - 39 = 3$$
$$30 + 3 = 33 \text{ (answer)}$$

Other Method:

$$72 - 40 = 32$$
$$40 - 39 = 1$$
$$32 + 1 = 33$$

Get the gist?

MULTIPLYING FRACTIONS

EXAMPLE 1

What is $3\frac{1}{2} \times 3\frac{2}{3}$?

Whenever you see something like this example, always write the two numbers as fractions. That is, write $3\frac{1}{2}$ as a fraction and write $3\frac{2}{3}$ as another fraction, then multiply.

Here's how to change $3\frac{1}{2}$ to a fraction:

To find the *numerator* for $3\frac{1}{2}$:

Then add

$3\frac{1}{2}$ $2 \times 3 + 1 = $ numerator

Multiply

To find the *denominator* for $3\frac{1}{2}$:

$$3\frac{1}{2} \to 2 = \text{denominator}$$

$$3\frac{1}{2} = \frac{2 \times 3 + 1}{2} = \frac{6 + 1}{2} = \frac{7}{2} = \frac{\text{numerator}}{\text{denominator}}$$

To convert $3\frac{2}{3}$ as a fraction, we follow the same method we used for $3\frac{1}{2}$:

Numerator:

Then add

Multiply

$3\frac{2}{3}$ $3 \times 3 + 2 = 11 = \text{numerator}$

Denominator:

$$3\frac{2}{3} \to 3 = \text{denominator}$$

$$3\frac{2}{3} = \frac{\text{numerator}}{\text{denominator}} = \frac{11}{3}$$

Now multiply:

$$3\frac{1}{2} \times 3\frac{2}{3} = \frac{7}{2} \times \frac{11}{3} = \frac{77}{6} = 12\frac{5}{6} \text{ (answer)}$$

EXAMPLE 2   What is $3\frac{1}{2} \times 6$?

$$3\frac{1}{2} = \frac{6 + 1}{2} = \frac{7}{2}$$

$$6 = \frac{6}{1}$$

So:

$$3\frac{1}{2} \times 6 = \frac{7}{2} \times 6 = \frac{7}{\cancel{2}} \times \cancel{6}^{\,3} = 21 \text{ (answer)}$$

After you have shown your child the math shortcuts just presented, have him or her try the following exercises.

$\dfrac{37}{21}$

EXERCISES

Questions 1–3. Which is greater?

1 $\dfrac{3}{7}$ or $\dfrac{6}{15}$ 45   42

2 $\dfrac{3}{4}$ or $\dfrac{4}{5}$ 15   16

3 $\dfrac{2}{3}$ or $\dfrac{7}{9}$ 14   21

Questions 4–5. Add:

4 $\dfrac{3}{7} + \dfrac{4}{3}$ 28 $\dfrac{9}{21} + \dfrac{28}{21}$

5 $\dfrac{2}{3} + \dfrac{3}{4}$

$\dfrac{8}{12} + \dfrac{9}{12}$ $\dfrac{17}{12}$

Questions 6–8. Subtract:

6 $\dfrac{2}{3} - \dfrac{1}{4}$

7 $\dfrac{3}{4} - \dfrac{2}{3}$

2

8 $2 - \dfrac{2}{5}$

Questions 9–10. Multiply:

9 $\dfrac{7}{8} \times \dfrac{8}{25}$

10 $\dfrac{2}{5} \times \dfrac{25}{16}$ $\dfrac{5}{8}$

Questions 11–14. Find what percent these fractions are:

11 $\dfrac{14}{25}$ · 4   56% $\dfrac{56}{100}$

12 $\dfrac{3}{250}$ 83%

13 $\dfrac{1}{50}$ $\dfrac{2}{100}$ 2%

14 $\dfrac{4}{5}$ 80%

Questions 15–17. Subtract:

15 1,15 − 99

16 63 − 49

17 202 − 99

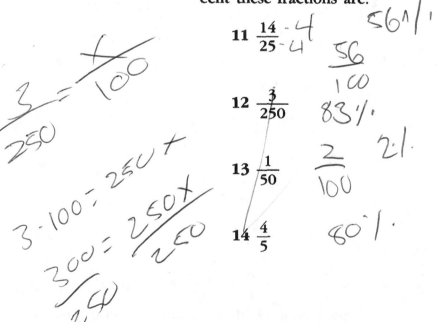

$\begin{array}{r} 0.83 \\ 300\overline{)2500} \\ 2400 \\ 1000 \\ 900 \end{array}$

$250\overline{)300}$

$\begin{array}{r} 83 \\ 3\overline{)250} \\ 24 \end{array}$

10

$\dfrac{3}{250} = \dfrac{x}{100}$

$3 \cdot 100 = 250x$

$300 = 250x$

$\dfrac{300}{250} = \dfrac{250x}{250}$

Questions 18–21. Multiply:

18 $1\frac{1}{2} \times 1\frac{1}{2}$

19 $2\frac{1}{3} \times 2\frac{2}{3}$

20 $4\frac{1}{4} \times 5$

21 $7,010 \times 500$

Questions 22–23. Divide:

22 40 by .25

23 700 by 50

35000

7000 ✗ 500

3500000

SOLUTIONS

1

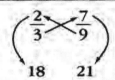

$$\left(\frac{3}{7} \times \frac{6}{15}\right)$$

$$45 \quad\quad 42$$

45 is greater than 42, so $\frac{3}{7}$ is greater than $\frac{6}{15}$.

2

$$\left(\frac{3}{4} \times \frac{4}{5}\right)$$

$$15 \quad\quad 16$$

$\frac{3}{4}$ is less than $\frac{4}{5}$ since 15 is less than 16.

3

$$\left(\frac{2}{3} \times \frac{7}{9}\right)$$

$$18 \quad\quad 21$$

$\frac{2}{3}$ is less than $\frac{7}{9}$ since 18 is less than 21.

4

$$\frac{3}{7} + \frac{4}{3} = \frac{(3 \times 3) + (7 \times 4)}{21}$$

$$= \frac{9 + 28}{21}$$

$$= \frac{37}{21} = 1\frac{16}{21}$$

5

$$\frac{2}{3} + \frac{3}{4} = \frac{(4 \times 2) + (3 \times 3)}{12}$$

$$= \frac{8 + 9}{12}$$

$$= \frac{17}{12} = 1\frac{5}{12}$$

6

$$\frac{2}{3} - \frac{1}{4} = \frac{(4 \times 2) - (3 \times 1)}{12}$$

$$= \frac{8 - 3}{12}$$

$$= \frac{5}{12}$$

7

$$\frac{3}{4} - \frac{2}{3} = \frac{(3 \times 3) - (4 \times 2)}{12}$$

$$= \frac{9 - 8}{12}$$

$$= \frac{1}{12}$$

8

$$2 - \frac{2}{5} = \frac{2}{1} - \frac{2}{5}$$

$$= \frac{10 - 2}{5}$$

$$= \frac{8}{5} = 1\frac{3}{5}$$

9

$$\frac{7}{8} \times \frac{8}{25} =$$

$$\frac{7}{\cancel{8}_1} \times \frac{\cancel{8}^1}{25} = \frac{7}{25}$$

10

$$\frac{2}{5} \times \frac{25}{16} =$$

$$\overset{1}{\cancel{\underset{}{2}}} \times \frac{\overset{5}{\cancel{25}}}{\underset{8}{\cancel{16}}} = \frac{5}{8}$$

11 $$\frac{14}{25} \times \frac{4}{4} = \frac{56}{100} = 56\%$$

12 $$\frac{3}{250} \times \frac{4}{4} = \frac{12}{1,000} = \frac{1.2}{100} = 1.2\%$$

13 $$\frac{1}{50} \times \frac{2}{2} = \frac{2}{100} = 2\%$$

14 $$\frac{4}{5} \times \frac{20}{20} = \frac{80}{100} = 80\%$$

15
$$115 - 100 = 15$$
$$100 - 99 = 1$$
$$15 + 1 = 16$$

16
$$63 - 50 = 13$$
$$50 - 49 = 1$$
$$13 + 1 = 14$$

17
$$202 - 100 = 102$$
$$100 - 99 = 1$$
$$102 + 1 = 103$$

OR

$$202 - 102 = 100$$
$$102 - 99 = 3$$
$$100 + 3 = 103$$

18 $$1\frac{1}{2} = \frac{2 + 1}{2} = \frac{3}{2}$$

$$1\frac{1}{2} \times 1\frac{1}{2} = \frac{3}{2} \times \frac{3}{2} = \frac{9}{4} = 2\frac{1}{4}$$

19

$$2\frac{1}{3} = \frac{6+1}{3} = \frac{7}{3}$$

$$2\frac{2}{3} = \frac{6+2}{3} = \frac{8}{3}$$

$$2\frac{1}{3} \times 2\frac{2}{3} = \frac{7}{3} \times \frac{8}{3} = \frac{56}{9} = 6\frac{2}{9}$$

20

$$4\frac{1}{4} = \frac{(4 \times 4) + 1}{4} = \frac{17}{4}$$

$$5 = \frac{5}{1}$$

$$4\frac{1}{4} \times 5 = \frac{17}{4} \times \frac{5}{1} = \frac{85}{4} = 21\frac{1}{4}$$

21

$$7{,}010 \times 500 =$$

$$7{,}010 \times 500 \times \frac{2}{2} =$$

$$\frac{7{,}010 \times 1{,}000}{2} = \frac{7{,}010{,}000}{2}$$

$$= 3{,}505{,}000$$

22

$$\frac{40}{.25} = \frac{40}{.25} \times \frac{4}{4} = \frac{160}{1.0} = 160$$

23

$$\frac{700}{50} = \frac{700}{50} \times \frac{2}{2} = \frac{1{,}400}{100}$$

$$= \frac{1{,}400}{100} = 14$$

The Thirty-two Basic Math Problems for Grades 6 to 9

Here are thirty-two of the most basic math problems (for grades 6 to 9), which your child should know how to solve. After your child finishes these, check to see whether they were done correctly by comparing his or her approaches and answers with the approaches and answers given following these questions. However, don't expect your child to have every answer, or even to be able to do all of the problems, especially the last ones, because your child may not have learned in school some of the material applicable to those questions.

1 $\begin{array}{r} 5.75 \\ \times \quad 6 \\ \hline \end{array}$

2 $\begin{array}{r} 6{,}613 \\ -\ 5{,}541 \\ \hline \end{array}$

3 $10{,}000 - 212$

4 $\dfrac{5}{6}$ (write as decimal)

5 $5\,\overline{)\,2{,}515}$

6 $\dfrac{1}{16} \times \dfrac{3}{4} =$

7 $770{,}007 + 70{,}770 =$

8 $\dfrac{273}{13} =$

9 $\dfrac{3\,(44 - 25)}{9} =$

10 $\dfrac{4}{7} - \dfrac{3}{14} =$

11 $724 + 31 + 5 + 816 + 72 =$

12 $5{,}710 \times 8 =$

13 1 quarter, 2 dimes, and 3 nickels = how many half dollars and dimes?

14 $4 - 3.09 =$

15 $5 \times \dfrac{4}{7} =$

16 $\dfrac{3}{4} + \dfrac{4}{5} =$

17 $581 + 1.7 + 12.21 =$

18 If $y = 2p + 3$ and $p = 2$, then $y =$

19 The ratio of 3 to 15 is equal to the ratio of 8 to what?

20 $\quad$ 55 minutes   51 seconds
$+$ 20 minutes   52 seconds

$=$ how many hours, minutes, seconds.

21 $9\dfrac{1}{4} \div 3\dfrac{1}{4} =$

22 $0.4 =$ what percent?

23 $2\dfrac{1}{5} \times \dfrac{4}{5} =$

24 $\quad\quad 7.21$
$\times \quad .09$

25 $.00071 \times 100 =$

26 $7 - \dfrac{2}{3} =$

27 $7.62 \div 30 =$

28 $\dfrac{-4 + 6}{-5} =$

29 100 grams is how many kilograms (1 kilogram $=$ 1,000 grams)?

30 $(-2)^2 + 4^2(5) =$

31 $\sqrt{25} =$

32 $3(26 - 21) =$

Solutions to the Thirty-two Basic Math Problems

↙ **two decimal places to left**

1
$$\begin{array}{r} 5.75 \\ \times\ \ \ \ 6 \\ \hline \boxed{34.50} \end{array}$$

↖ **two decimal places to left**

2
$$\begin{array}{r} {}^5\!\!\!\!6\!\!\!/13 \\ -\ 5541 \\ \hline \boxed{1{,}072} \end{array}$$

3
$$\begin{array}{r} {}^{09}\ {}^{99} \\ 1\!\!\!/0\!\!\!/,\!0\!\!\!/0\!\!\!/0 \\ -\ \ \ \ 212 \\ \hline \boxed{9{,}788} \end{array}$$

4
$$\begin{array}{r} .8333 \ldots \text{ all of the rest are 3's} \\ 6)\overline{5.0000} \\ \underline{48\text{xxx}} \\ 20 \\ \underline{18} \\ 20 \\ \underline{18} \\ 20 \end{array}$$

5
$$\begin{array}{r} \boxed{503} \\ 5)\overline{2515} \\ \underline{25\text{x}} \\ 015 \\ \underline{15} \\ 0 \end{array}$$

6    $\dfrac{1}{16} \times \dfrac{3}{4} = \dfrac{3}{16 \times 4} = \boxed{\dfrac{3}{64}}$

7
$$\begin{array}{r} {}^1 \\ 770{,}007 \\ +\ \ 70{,}770 \\ \hline \boxed{840{,}777} \end{array}$$

8
$$\begin{array}{r} \boxed{21} \\ 13)\overline{273} \\ \underline{26\text{x}} \\ 13 \end{array}$$

9 $\dfrac{3(44-25)}{9} = \dfrac{\cancel{3}\,(44-25)}{\underset{3}{\cancel{9}}}$

$= \dfrac{44-25}{3}$

$= \boxed{\dfrac{19}{3} \text{ or } 6\dfrac{1}{3}}$

10 $\dfrac{4}{7} - \dfrac{3}{14}$

$\dfrac{4}{7} \times \dfrac{2}{2} = \dfrac{8}{14}$

$\dfrac{8}{14} - \dfrac{3}{14} = \boxed{\dfrac{5}{14}}$

11
$$
\begin{array}{r}
\overset{11}{724} \\
31 \\
5 \\
816 \\
+\ \ 72 \\
\hline
\boxed{1{,}648}
\end{array}
$$

12
$$
\begin{array}{r}
5{,}710 \\
\times\ ^{5}\ \ 8 \\
\hline
\boxed{45{,}680}
\end{array}
$$

13

1 quarter	=	$\overset{1}{2}5$¢
2 dimes	=	20¢
3 nickels	=	15¢
	+	
		60¢

60¢ $= 50$¢ $+ 10$¢

$= \boxed{1 \text{ half dollar } + 1 \text{ dime}}$

14
$$
\begin{array}{r}
\overset{3}{\cancel{4}}\overset{9}{\cancel{.0}}0 \\
-\ 3.09 \\
\hline
\boxed{0.91}
\end{array}
$$

15 $5 \times \dfrac{4}{7} = \dfrac{5}{1} \times \dfrac{4}{7} = \dfrac{20}{7}$

$$\boxed{\dfrac{20}{7} \text{ or } 2\dfrac{6}{7}}$$

16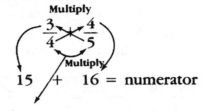

15 $/$ + 16 = numerator

$4 \times 5 = 20$ = denominator

$$\boxed{\dfrac{31}{20} \text{ or } 1\dfrac{11}{20}}$$

17
```
   581.00
     1.70
    12.21
```
$$\boxed{594.91}$$

18 $y = 2p + 3$
$p = 2$ (substitute 2 for p)

$y = 2p + 3$
$\quad\quad\quad\nwarrow 2$ (since $p = 2$)
$y = 2(2) + 3$
$\quad = 4 + 3 = \boxed{7}$

19 $\dfrac{3}{15} = \dfrac{8}{?}$
$\uparrow$ reduce

$\dfrac{1}{5} = \dfrac{8}{?}$

Cross-multiply:

$\left(\dfrac{1}{5} \times \dfrac{8}{?}\right.$
$? = 5 \times 8$
$\quad = 40$
$? = \boxed{40}$

20

$$55 \text{ minutes} \quad 51 \text{ seconds}$$
$$\underline{+\ 20 \text{ minutes} \quad 52 \text{ seconds}}$$
$$75 \text{ minutes} \ 103 \text{ seconds}$$
$$\downarrow \qquad\qquad \downarrow$$
$$60 \text{ minutes} \quad 60 \text{ seconds}$$
$$+\ 15 \text{ minutes} + 43 \text{ seconds}$$
$$\downarrow \qquad\qquad \downarrow$$
$$1 \text{ hour, } 15 \text{ minutes} \quad 1 \text{ minute, } 43 \text{ seconds}$$

$$\boxed{1 \text{ hour, } 16 \text{ minutes, } 43 \text{ seconds}}$$

21 $\quad 9\dfrac{1}{4} \div 3\dfrac{1}{4} =$

(express in simple form)

$$\dfrac{37}{4} \div \dfrac{13}{4} =$$

invert to multiply

$$\dfrac{37}{4} \times \dfrac{4}{13} =$$

$$\dfrac{37}{\cancel{4}} \times \dfrac{\cancel{4}}{13} = \boxed{\dfrac{37}{13}}$$

$$= \boxed{2\dfrac{11}{13}}$$

22 $\quad\quad\quad 0.4 = \dfrac{4}{10}$

$$\dfrac{4}{10} \times \dfrac{10}{10} = \dfrac{40}{100} = \boxed{40\%}$$

23 $\quad 2\dfrac{1}{5} \times \dfrac{4}{5} =$

express as simple fraction

$$\dfrac{11}{5} \times \dfrac{4}{5} =$$

$$\dfrac{11 \times 4}{5 \times 5} = \dfrac{44}{25} = \boxed{1\dfrac{19}{25}}$$

24

$$\begin{array}{r} 7.21 \\ \times\ \ .09 \end{array}$$ ← 2 decimal places

← 2 decimal places

7.21   **must be 4 decimal places in answer (2 × 2)**

$$\begin{array}{r} ^1\ .09 \\ \hline 6489 \end{array}$$

.6489.

$$= \boxed{.6489}$$

25

┌─── **5 decimal places to left**

↓.00071

$$\begin{array}{r} \times\ \ \ \ \ 100 \\ \hline 00.07100 \end{array}$$

← **5 decimal places to left**

$$\boxed{.071}$$

26

$$7 - \frac{2}{3} =$$

$$\frac{7}{1} - \frac{2}{3} =$$

Multiply

$$\frac{7}{1} \diagdown\!\!\!\diagup \frac{2}{3} =$$

Multiply

$$\frac{21 - 2}{3} = \frac{19}{3} = \boxed{6\frac{1}{3}}$$

27

$$\begin{array}{r} .254 \\ 30\overline{)7.62000} \\ \underline{60}xx \\ 162 \\ \underline{150} \\ 120 \\ \underline{120} \\ 0 \end{array}$$ $$\boxed{.254}$$

28 $$\frac{-4 +6}{-5} = \frac{+2}{-5} = \boxed{-\frac{2}{5}}$$

29   1 Kilogram = 1,000 grams

Divide both sides of the equation by 10:

$$\frac{1}{10} \text{ Kilogram} = \frac{1}{10} (1,000) \text{ grams} = 100 \text{ grams}$$

So 100 grams = $\boxed{\dfrac{1}{10} \text{ Kilogram}}$

30 $(-2)^2 + 4^2(5) =$

$(-2)^2 = -2 \times -2 = +4$

$4^2 = 4 \times 4 = 16$

So $(-2)^2 + 4^2(5) = 4 + 16(5)$

$$\begin{array}{r} 16 \\ \times\ \ 5 \\ \hline 80 \end{array}$$

So $4 + 16(5) = 4 + 80 = \boxed{84}$

31 $\sqrt{25} = \boxed{5}$ since $5 \times 5 = 25$

32 $3(26-21) = 3(5) = 3 \times 5 = \boxed{15}$
$\qquad\quad \uparrow$
$\quad\ 26-21=5$

Appendix A: Hot Prefixes and Roots

Here is a list of the most important prefixes and roots that impart a certain meaning or feeling. They can be instant clues to the meanings of more than 110,000 words.

PREFIXES WHICH MEAN TO, WITH, BETWEEN, OR AMONG

PREFIX	MEANING	EXAMPLES
ad, ac, af, an, ap, ap, as, at	to, toward	adapt—to fit into adhere—to stick to attract—to draw near
com, con, co, col	with, together	combine—to bring together contact—to touch together collect—to bring together co-worker—one who works together with another worker
in, il, ir, im	into	inject—to put into impose—to force into illustrate—to put into example irritate—to put into discomfort
inter	between, among	international—among nations interact—to act among the people
pro	forward, going ahead	proceed—to go forward promote—to move forward

PREFIXES WHICH MEAN BAD

PREFIX	MEANING	EXAMPLES
mal	wrong, bad	malady—illness malevolent—bad malfunction—bad functioning
mis	wrong, badly	mistreat—to treat badly mistake—to get wrong

PREFIXES WHICH MEAN AWAY FROM, NOT, OR AGAINST

PREFIX	MEANING	EXAMPLES
ab	away from	absent—not to be present, away abscond—to run away

| de, dis | away from, down, the opposite of, apart, not | depart—to go away from
decline—to turn down
dislike—not to like
dishonest—not honest
distant—apart |

PREFIXES WHICH MEAN AWAY FROM, NOT, OR AGAINST

PREFIX	MEANING	EXAMPLES
ex, e, ef	out, from	exit—to go out eject—to throw out efface—to rub out, erase
in, il, ir, im	not	inactive—not active impossible—not possible ill-mannered—not mannered irreversible—not reversible
non	not	nonsense—no sense nonstop—having no stops
un	not	unhelpful—not helpful uninterested—not interested
anti	against	anti-freeze—a substance used to prevent freezing anti-social—refers to someone who's not social
ob	against, in front of	obstacle—something that stands in the way of obstinate—inflexible

PREFIXES WHICH DENOTE DISTANCE

PREFIX	MEANING	EXAMPLES
circum	around	circumscribe—to write or inscribe in a circle circumspect—to watch around or be very careful
equ, equi	equal, the same	equalize—to make equal equitable—fair, equal
post	after	postpone—to do after postmortem—after death

pre	before	preview—a viewing that goes before another viewing prehistorical—before written history
trans	across	transcontinental—across the continent transit—act of going across
re	back, again	retell—to tell again recall—to call back, to remember
sub	under	subordinate—under something else subconcious—under the conscious
super	over, above	superimpose—to put something over something else superstar—a star greater than other stars
un, uni	one	unity—oneness unanimous—sharing one view unidirectional—having one direction

ROOTS

ROOT	MEANING	EXAMPLES
cap, capt, cept, ceive	to take, to hold	captive—one who is held receive—to take capable—to be able to take hold of things concept—an idea or thought held in mind
cred	to believe	credible—believable credit—belief, trust
curr, curs, cours	to run	current—now in progress, running cursor—a moveable indicator recourse—to run for aid
dic, dict	to say	indicate—to say by demonstrating diction—verbal saying
duc, duct	to lead	induce—to lead to action aqueduct—a pipe or waterway that leads water somewhere

fac, fic, fect, fy	to make, to do	facile—easy to do fiction—something that has been made up satisfy—to make happy affect—to make a change in
jec, ject	to throw	project—to put forward trajectory—a path of an object that has been thrown
mit, mis	to send	admit—to send in missile—something that gets sent through the air
pon, pos,	to place	transpose—to place across compose—to put into place many parts deposit—to place in something
scrib, script	to write	describe—to write or tell about scripture—a written tablet
spec, spic	to look	specimen—an example to look at inspect—to look over
ten, tain	to hold	maintain—to hold up or keep retentive—holding
ven, vent	to come	advent—a coming convene—to come together

Appendix B: The Dangers of National School Entrance Testing

Are the national testing companies—who test hundreds of thousands of students each year—actually destroying our kids' potential and enthusiasm for learning? This book develops and restores that potential and passion, allowing the student to score markedly higher even though the tests may be flawed.

Here is a question on an actual Secondary School Admission test (SSAT), the test for private high school entrance. This question has also appeared in the company's official test-preparation guide for more than ten years. It is one of many questions with such ambiguities.

See if you or your child can correctly answer this question.

What is the meaning of the word POLISH?

(A) burnish (B) lighten (C) wax (D) coat (E) clean

The correct answer (according to the testing company) is (A) burnish.
But POLISH as can be seen in any dictionary to mean smooth, brighten, or refine, making all the choices correct!

The Dangers of Ambiguity

When a student who is already anxious about taking a test attempts to answer not one but a series of questions that have ambiguous answers or cannot be answered, the student will get so befuddled that he will do poorly on the rest of the test. However, if a student is armed with the strategies in this book, his confidence will be so heightened that he will see through these flaws and not get discouraged.

Here are some of the erroneous questions that have appeared on the actual SSAT and are also in the official book of the SSAT, *SSAT: Preparing and Applying*. These are taken directly from the Upper Level Practice Test II.

Find the meaning of:

28. ANDROGYNOUS
    (A) alien
    (B) bisexual
    (C) metallic
    (D) underground
    (E) insecticide
SSAT Answer: B

The definition of androgynous is both male and female in one, not necessarily bisexual!

49. Anesthesiologist is to sedate as
    (A) optometrist is to glasses
    (B) hypnotist is to spell
    (C) agronomist is to plant
    (D) economist is to prediction
    (E) humanist is to people
SSAT Answer: B

Any person who knows even little about analogies would answer this one as follows: "The purpose of an Anesthesiologist is to sedate as the purpose of a hypnotist is to spell?" It is elementary to realize that "sedate" should not have been used as a verb. In fact, the word after "is to" in the stem of the choice (sedate) has to be the same part of speech as all the words after "is to" in the choices. Note that in Choice A, glasses is a noun, in Choice B spell is a noun, and the word after "is to" in the choices C, D, and E are nouns. This is a totally erroneous analogy question.

45. Happy is to worried as
(A) please is to passion
(B) ecstatic is to panicked
(C) cheerful is to confused
(D) glow is to glare
(E) lively is to dull

SSAT Answer: B

Here the test writer used the following: Happy is to ecstatic as worried is to panicked. The sequence is incorrect for analogies. The question stem should have been "Happy is to ecstatic" and the correct choice should have been (B) worried is to panicked

3. PREVALENT
(A) ahead
(B) common
(C) elected
(D) overlooked
(E) collected

SSAT Answer: B

Prevalent is defined as "widely existent," or "generally accepted."
"Common" does not fit.

4. PATHETIC
(A) guidance
(B) trash
(C) poor
(D) direction
(E) wretched

SSAT Answer: E

PATHETIC is an adjective and Choices A, D are nouns. Choice B is either a verb or noun. Choices A , D and B must be modified.

Actual SSAT Questions

Here are actual SSAT questions that many people have asked me how to solve because they thought they were too difficult and felt it was unfair of the testing company to use them. These questions are not ambiguous, but there are powerful strategies you can use to answer each question. Learning these strategies—all of which appear in this book—will give your child the confidence to get through the test no matter what the test is like, leveling the playing field for everyone.

Find the closest meaning to the word in capitalized letters:

Q. DECEIVE: (A) alter (B) examine (C) astonish (D) mislead (E) pretend

A. (D) See Appendix A—these prefixes and roots will give you the meaning of more than 150,000 words! Since the prefix DE means away from, it is negative. So lets look for a choice that gives the feeling of being negative. The only choice is (D) mislead, since the prefix mis is also negative. (See Vocabulary Strategy 1.)

(For the following vocab questions, strategies and additional examples can be found in Vocabulary Strategies 1 and 2.)

Q. COMPASSION: (A) sympathy (B) honor (C) shyness (D) amazement (E) courage

A. (A) Associate words with other words—another strategy you should have learned in this book. Look for some part of the word that you understand. You've heard of PASSION. Now look for a choice that has some emotion in it. Choice A is the best one.

Q. REMINISCENCE: (A) limitation (B) contraction (C) moderation (D) recollection (E) removal

A. (D) What word seems to be part of or associated with REMINISCENCE? REMIND. Choice D is the best one.

Q. PROPHESY: (A) defeat (B) annoy (C) foretell (D) testify (E) prompt

A. (C) Look for the prefix to give a clue: PRO which means forward or ahead. Which choice looks like it means something forward? (C) foretell.

Q. ASCERTAIN: (A) give up (B) add to (C) join with (D) follow after (E) find out

A. (E) What word in ASCERTAIN do you recognize: CERTAIN! So look for a choice that is associated closely with the word CERTAIN. Wouldn't it be (E) find out?

Q. RESIDUAL: (A) surrounded by (B) leftover (C) responsive to (D) finished (E) runaway

A. (B) The prefix RE means "back." What choice has something to do with "back?" (B) leftover.

Q. ADJUNCT: (A) endeavor (B) impatience (C) ridicule (D) compulsion (E) accessory

A. (E) The prefix AD means "toward" or "to." What does JUNCT make you think of. Perhaps JUNCTION or JOIN? What joins something? (E) accessory

Q. ENTOURAGE: (A) attendants (B) journeys (C) schedules (D) displays (E) awards

A. (A) This is a difficult one to figure out, but think of TOUR in ENTOURAGE. So you could eliminate choices D and E. You are left to choose either A, B or C, and now you're chances of getting it correct are one in three, which is better than one in five. (The correct answer is (A) attendants.)

Q. IMPASSE (A) deadlock (B) distortion (C) variance (D) neutrality (E) recklessness

A. (A) The prefix IM usually means "not." Look at the word PASS in IMPASSE. So you can figure out that the word might mean "not to be able to pass." So look for a word that means to "stop" or "prevent from passing," etc. You can see that (A) deadlock fits the bill.

Let's look at some analogies. (For the following analogies, strategies and additional examples can be found in Analogies.)

Q. Immaculate is to dirt as
    (A) indecent is to person
    (B) inclement is to rain
    (C) immortal is to heaven
    (D) impious is to volume
    (E) innocent is to guilt

A. (E) Let's say you don't know what the meaning of "immaculate" is. Since it must relate to "dirt," let's take a guess and say "immaculate" may mean "not dirty." So let's see if we can find an opposite in the choices. Choice E is the only one.

Q. Intangible is to touching as
    (A) incisive is to cutting
    (B) inadvertent is to seeing
    (C) inaudible is to hearing
    (D) inarticulate is to reading
    (E) incendiary is to burning

A. (C) Just as in the answer to the first question, if you don't know the meaning of intangible, you could think of it as an opposite to touching and see if you get an opposite in one of the choices. Choice C looks like the one.

Q. Map is to land as
    (A) negative is to print
    (B) diagram is to machine
    (C) camera is to film
    (D) crayon is to paint
    (E) lens is to glass

A. Let's get a meaningful sentence that relates map and land. (This is a powerful strategy for cracking analogies.) You can say a map tells you how to get around the land. Now look for a choice that, when you put the words of the choice in the same sentence form, you get a match.Look at Choice A: a negative tells you how to get around a print. No.
Look at Choice B: a diagram tells you how to get around a machine. Possible.
Look at Choice C: a camera tells you how to get around a film. No.
Look at Choice D: a crayon tells you how to get around a paint. No.
Look at Choice E: a lens tells you how to get around a glass. No.
Choice B is best.

Q. Recalcitrant is to obedience as insolent is to
    (A) luck
    (B) stealth
    (C) fear
    (D) respect
    (E) anger

A. (D) Since the "Re" in "Recalcitrant" means "back," it has a negative connotation, so let's assume that "recalcitrant" means the opposite of "obedience." Now let's look for an opposite to "insolent." Let's assume that the "in" means "not" and the word is negative. So look for a positive choice that somewhat relates to behavior. It is Choice D.

Q. Obsessed is to interested as
   (A) weak is to ill
   (B) ferocious is to unexpected
   (C) pristine is to clean
   (D) moist is to humid
   (E) fashionable is to new

A. (C) What could the word "obsessed" mean in relation to the word "interested?" Let's say it is a level of how interested you are. Let's assume that level is "very" interested. Notice that Choices A, B, D, and E do not have this relation. So even if you didn't know that the word "pristine" meant "very clean," you could have still eliminated all the other choices to get Choice C.

Q. Variegated is to color as
   (A) polymorphous is to shape
   (B) amorphous is to skeleton
   (C) quadrilateral is to polygon
   (D) aeronautic is to plane
   (E) celestial is to planet

A. (A) Even if you don't know the meaning of "variegated," you can associate "vary" with that word. So if things are varied, there are many colors. Let's look for a choice that shows many of something else. "Poly" means many, so (A) is the best choice.

Math—All of these questions can be answered quickly with powerful strategies in this book.

Q. Of the following, 0.49 X 81 is closest to
   (A) $\frac{1}{2}$ of 80
   (B) $\frac{1}{2}$ of 90
   (C) $\frac{1}{4}$ of 80
   (D) $\frac{1}{4}$ of 90
   (E) 4 times 80

A. (A) The key word here is "closest to." So instead of multiplying 0.49×81, let's approximate 0.49 to 0.5—which is $\frac{1}{2}$—and 81 to 80. Thus you can see that Choice A is correct. (See Math Strategy 3.)

Q. All of the following are greater than $\frac{1}{2}$ EXCEPT
   (A) $\frac{101}{200}$
   (B) $\frac{17}{33}$
   (C) $\frac{7}{12}$
   (D) $\frac{600}{1000}$
   (E) $\frac{24}{50}$

A. (E) Whenever you have to test all the choices, start with Choice E. You should immediately connect $\frac{1}{2}$ with $\frac{24}{50}$. $\frac{1}{2} = \frac{25}{50}$, so you can see that the quantity in Choice E is less than $\frac{1}{2}$. (See Math Strategy 5.)

Q. For what price is 20 percent off the same as $20 off?
   (A) $1
   (B) $10
   (C) $100
   (D) $1000
   (E) it is never the same.

A. (C) Try the choices, starting with Choice D. 20% of $1000 is $200. $200 off $1000 gives you $800. For Choice D, $20 off $1000 results in $980. Look at Choice C: 20% of $100 is $20. $20 off $100 is $80. For Choice C, $20 off $100 is also $80. Thus Choice C is correct. (See Math Strategies 5 and 2.)

Q. If $\frac{1}{4}$ N = 12, then $\frac{1}{2}$ N =
   (A) 3
   (B) 6
   (C) 24
   (D) 48
   (E) 96

A. (C) How do I relate $\frac{1}{4}$ with $\frac{1}{2}$? $\frac{1}{4} = \frac{1}{2} \times \frac{1}{2}$. So $\frac{1}{4}$N = $\frac{1}{2} \times \frac{1}{2}$ N = 12.
Multiply by 2 and we get: $2 \times \frac{1}{2} \times \frac{1}{2}$ N = 2 X 12 = 24. (See Math Strategy 1.)

Q. Of the following, 15 percent of $8.95 is closest to
   (A) $1.95
   (B) $1.75
   (C) $1.50
   (D) $1.35
   (E) $1.00

A. (D) Look at the key word "closest." Round up $8.95 to $9.00. Remember that 15% of a quantity is 10% of the quantity + 1/2 that result. So 15% of $9 is 10% of $9, which equals $0.90, then + $\frac{1}{2}$ of that amount, which is $\frac{1}{2}$ + 0.90 = 0.45. So the result is $1.35. This is a good way to figure out a 15% tip at a restaurant! (See Math Strategies 3 and 2.)

Q. John has x dollars. Ann has $5 more than John. If Ann gives John $10, then, in terms of x, how many dollars will Ann have?
   (A) x – 15
   (B) x – 10
   (C) x – 5
   (D) x + 5
   (E) x + 15

A. (C) Translate verbal to math. Let J = x. "Has" translates to =, "more" translates to +. Therefore, "Ann has $5 more than John" translates to A = 5 + J. If Ann gives John $10, Ann has A-10. Since A = 5 + J,   A –10 = 5 + J –10.
A –10 = J - 5 = x – 5 (See Math Strategy 2.)

Q. A store regularly sells books at 20% off the list price. At a sale its regular prices are reduced 10 percent. The sale price is what percent of the list price?
   (A) 30%
   (B) 70%
   (C) 72%
   (D) 79%
   (E) 85%

A. (C) Imagine an item at the bookstore that costs an even $100. 20% off $100 gives you $80, and thus the price of the item is $80. Since at a sale the store's regular price is reduced 10%, let's take 10% off $80. That gives $8. So the final price is $80 - $8 = $72. The question asks: the sale price is what percent of the list price. We had calculated that the sale price is $72. The list price is $100. Translate "is" to =, "what" to x, "percent" to /100, and "of" to X (times).

The sale price	is	what	percent	of	list price
$72	=	x	/100	X	$100

Thus 72 = x/100 X (100) = x, so x = 72. (See Math Strategy 2.)

About the Author

Gary R. Gruber, PhD, is recognized nationally as the leading expert on the SAT, test-taking methods, and critical thinking skills. His books on test taking and critical thinking skills have sold more than seven million copies.

NOTES

NOTES

NOTES

NOTES

NOTES

NOTES